WITHOUT BRUISES

Jillian "JJ" Simmons

DEDICATION

To CD and LS; you both have such beautiful spirits. I can't begin to thank you enough for sharing, listening and carrying me during one of my most fragile times. I love you both very much.

ACKNOWLEDGEMENTS

Thanks to my beloved father, Alani Simmons, Quiana LaRae, Danielle Fanfair, Emma J, and Dr. Hank Roubicek for their inspiration, knowledge, and help in creating this book.

"In emotionally abusive relationships, one party systematically controls the other by undermining his or her confidence, worthiness, growth, trust, or emotional stability, or by provoking fear or shame to manipulate or exploit...In some respects, emotional abuse is more devastating than physical violence, due to the greater likelihood that victims will blame themselves."

Steven Stosny, Ph.D.
Psychology Today
February 23, 2013

CONTENTS

FOREWORD

Words, behavior, and even our very presence are forms of communication. Human beings have been given this remarkable gift, this ability to impart love, wisdom and life-sustaining knowledge to one another in ways that no other species can. Effective communication enables us to nurture strong children, cultivate relationships that nourish healthy families and promote productive communities.

I have always been enamored with communication to the masses. From the very first time I was given a transistor radio as a gift from my mother at the age of eight, I knew that my future would include sharing information with my people, using the power of radio. I would listen to deejays like Wolfman Jack and others and witness the power they had to inform and entertain, and I understood that communication was a great equalizer, for he who owns the medium controls the message.

At sixteen, I found myself pregnant with my son, and my mother required that I set-up my own living arrangements. I was forced to think about someone other than myself. I had to think about this innocent child who now relied on me for everything. I had to confront myself and was forced use communication to create my own narrative. My "self talk" was full of stories about my ability to make it on my own, about my value as a single mother and about the gift of being blessed with a child. I had to encourage myself to make positive choices from the core of who I am, to seize the opportunity to love and prioritize my son and not to allow either of us to become a statistic. I understood that what I said to myself was as important as what I said to others.

Armed with my mantra, "information is power," I worked to empower my community and affect change and established Radio One, which allows us to give voice and opportunity to those who do meaningful work and have information to share with the world. Many like Jillian "JJ" Simmons, a member of the Radio One family, who works with us sharing her life and light with our listeners. Now, "JJ" opens up her heart on the pages of her new book *Without Bruises,* an invitation and a roadmap to a life without the constant threat of danger that looms and lurks in a relationship characterized by abuse, controlling behavior, manipulation, and hurtful communication. "JJ" invites us into her journey of healing. She has courageously moved from a place of trauma and abuse and has done the work necessary to heal and overcome the fear of permanently ending a toxic relationship.

Now, as she communicates and shares her story on the pages of this book, she is creating a new pathway of expression in our human experience that can heal, soothe and unlock potential in others. That is why *Without Bruises* is so important. It allows her personal story to help us understand and identify forms of abuse. It is a glimmer of a light that illuminates the way out of the dark, harmful pattern that is formed in relationships that are toxic.

If you have picked up this book, you are reading with a community of people who simply want to love, be loved and live well.

That is the design, and the desire. So, before you begin reading, I wish you wellness, and it is my hope that JJ's courage would cause a contagious ripple effect that encourages present and future generations to invest in one another's health and wholeness by communicating love.

Cathy Hughes
Founder of Radio One Inc.

PROLOGUE

The word Playboy triggers different emotions for different people. For some, the word reminds them of a mischievous secret, discovered and prized through adolescence. For others, feelings of hurt, disdain, judgment. When I hear the word Playboy, I think immediately of my mother.

She was one of two black Playboy Bunnies in the members-only Playboy Club in our city during its heyday in the seventies and eighties. She was charming, beautiful, and hard working. She was a quintessential star. Most of my memories of her are around her constantly working. Because her appearance was her income, it was her primary concern.

After my parents' divorce, my mother gained custody of me, and we moved far from my father. I spent time with my dad every other weekend and more often during the summer. I remember spending lots of quality time with my father even before the divorce. The contrast between the life

I lived with my mom and what I experienced with my dad was so stark, it was shocking. Time with my father was loving, fun. He was a doting parent, never withholding his love and affection. My mother's style of parenting was critical, blunt and distant.

I don't recall hearing my mother tell me she loved me until after I became an adult. I do recall constantly feeling like she did not. I have more memories of being spoken to and treated with a harshness that motivated me to do everything I could to have one good day with her. I tried my hardest to figure out the combination that would unlock her heart, and result in a normal mother-daughter relationship.

I have not yet discovered it.

I find it interesting, and sad that so many of my friends and I have shared our parents' disciplinary tactics as jokes. We exchange stories of being cursed out, the targets of shoes and extension cords, laughing loudly, no one daring to call it what it is—abuse.

My desire to win my mother's love fueled a drive to endure years of manipulation, unnecessary drama, and major moments in my life punctuated by her angry fits. The cycle of abuse and effort between she and I would set the tone for my relationships going forward. I would later find myself bending to fit in between Stacey's emotional outbursts, demands, and critiques.

I entered adulthood with silent rules for how to navigate intimate connection. Be good enough. Figure out what makes a person happy and I will be happy. Work hard for love. I began my relationship with Stacey obeying these rules, and for too long refused to call the way he treated me abusive.

I set out on a journey to exchange my old rules for relationships for new practices that nurture me, heal me, and create a different experience for my young daughter. The unlearning process is hard. It is worth it. It became very dark before I caught a glimpse of the light. This book is the result and the artifact of the work of becoming free and is saving and enriching my life.

INTRODUCTION

The ardent pull that occurs between two people commonly results in a love affair. The affair can lead to deep, satisfying bonds, intense suffering or fall somewhere in between. When the affair leads to intense suffering, many women decide to avoid all romantic entanglements. Or, they view an invitation from a new prospect with suspicion or outright hostility. They have given up on the idea of finding a special someone to share life with. Don't do that. Even after what happened between Stacey and me, I still believe in true love.

I am not here to stop you from looking for that special someone. I'm here to tell you not to settle. It is important that you know what you want and need from a man before getting into a serious, committed relationship with him. Don't settle for less than what you need because you're lonely, he is handsome, you believe there are no good men left or anything else. Settling for less than you need or deserve leads to disaster.

I am about to tell you my story of a one-year relationship that I had with a guy named Stacey.

Why? I hope that you will learn from my mistakes and not sacrifice your precious time, emotions and self-esteem for lessons in love that everyone should ideally learn from their families.

Actually, young women should get the first lessons from their mothers. Unfortunately, my mother was never emotionally available for me due to problems of her own.

I had to learn how to love and be loved through trial and error.

So, the book you now hold in your hands is the story of my big, fat error.

I settled for Stacey even after it became obvious that he was a liar, a cheat and had some type of emotional problem. If ever there was a textbook case of emotional abuse, it was my love affair with Stacey.

After it was over, I set out to learn what had happened to me and eventually read a tremendous amount of material on the topic of Emotional Abuse. I will share that knowledge with you as well.

Emotional Abuse is defined as a hurtful pattern of controlling and manipulative behavior that often starts with negative comments about what you're wearing, who you spend time with, or other subtle forms of coercion. It can then lead to personal insults, public humiliation, and even financial abuse.

According to Safe Horizons, an organization that helps women escape from dangerous situations involving relationships, thousands of women are suffering in silence. When they seek help:

87% say that their abuser insulted their family and friends.

62% say that their abuser made them do humiliating things.

93% experienced economic abuse (prevented from working, harassment at work, ruining of credit score).

According to the National Coalition Against Domestic Violence, 7 out of 10 psychologically abused women display symptoms of PTSD or Depression.

So, kick back and read this emotional roller coaster.

Afterwards, go out and love, learn, love....but never, ever settle.

PART 1

HOW EMOTIONAL ABUSE CAN START

CHAPTER 1

SOMEBODY ELSE'S DREAM MAN

J acob was my high school sweetheart. During freshman year, I went to a predominantly black school that didn't have the best reputation as a place where students could achieve. I was popular and had the wrong friends. Then I was transferred to an all-white school. I hated it. I was miserable. My grades dropped and I felt alienated and isolated from everything and everyone who mattered. But Jacob was there through all of my ups and downs. He was a true romantic. He bought me flowers and Teddy Bears. When we went to fairs and festivals, he won prizes just for me. He was kind, loving, and had a sweet sort of innocence about him. I was his first sexual partner, so we also had a strong physical connection.

At first, our only apparent problem was that his family were Jehovah's Witnesses. That form of Christianity prohibited its members from getting involved in politics, affiliating with other religions, receiving blood transfusions, and so much more. Naturally, Jacob's mother wanted his girlfriend to be a member of their faith. He tried very hard to get her to like me, even though I had no plans to convert. She always appeared polite although I never gained her affection. After high school, Jacob got a job working at a General Motors plant. He was ecstatic because he could earn good money. In fact, he liked it so much he thought he'd even retire there. He could marry and have a family without dealing with financial worries. Home. Work. Wife. Kids. I wanted more from him. Maybe I wanted more from me. It was all he wanted out of life. I wanted a career in broadcasting. As I prepared to go away to college, I hoped that Jacob would change and become more ambitious in my absence.

After high school, I went to Georgia and attended Clark Atlanta University for one year, from 1996-1997. When I ran out of money for tuition, I came back to Ohio and stayed with a friend. Jacob got an apartment for me. He would have moved in with me but his mom had a fit when the idea came up. Jehovah's Witnesses do not live together without the benefit of marriage. I stayed there until I got my bearings and then moved to

Cincinnati, and took out some student loans to continue my college education. In the meantime, I kept sending my demo tape to a variety of stations around the country, hoping for a break. I knew all I needed was that chance to be inside the front door, because I knew my grit and talent would catapult me from there. And then it happened.

I moved to New York with no job and hustled for 3 months, motivated by faith in my dreams. Jacob was back in Ohio, living his dream of a simple life. I got a call in 2001 from New York's reputable WBLS. I couldn't believe it. Taking a job here would be like taking a baby step into the mouth of a giant. I ended up working with the fabulous Wendy Williams. To say it was a dream come true would be a gigantic understatement. I loved the job. Wendy hosted the afternoon show from 2-6pm and I hosted the evening show from 6-10pm. I remember listening to Wendy the first time the first day she hit the airwaves as a colleague of mine. I listened from home and I heard her say, "JJ is walking around here somewhere with her belly showing and a little belly ring." Actually I never had a belly ring, but I did wear some cut off shirts. The point is, I was so hype that Wendy was talking about me on the air! I was a true fan before working with her, but now I was awestruck. Wendy was a master of her craft. She would come in the studio with tons of magazines she had read and notebooks she had filled with ideas to talk about. The studio was always filled with roses sent by admiring fans---gestures of respect and appreciation. Wendy had her life set. Mine was just starting, professionally, but continued on the desperate relational path of no return.

I lived in Bed-Stuy Brooklyn with Trent, another radio personality. I cared for him a lot. He had hypnotic green eyes and a smile that was as engaging and contagious as the Pied Piper's flute. Unfortunately, as engaging as he was, he couldn't disengage from his ex. He was not over her. One day, I saw a postcard that came in the mail from this ex-girlfriend. And I read it. I had to. She said that she missed him, needed him, and loved him. I was appalled that she would send a postcard, knowing that I would see it. Then it struck me: "Why should I be appalled? She never knew I existed." A lot of conflict, empty apologies, lame explanations, and more ridiculous rhetoric than you'd ever imagine followed after the discovery.

Trent and I broke up over his deception. However, because I had nowhere to go, I stupidly continued to live with him for an additional three months, never uttering one word or acknowledging gesture to each other.

I had my dream job but I was miserable. Then, I began hating New York. I tolerated the city, knowing it was a way of getting ahead. But there was tumult and chaos in New York, largely because of September 11, so I made arrangements to leave and get home to Jacob.

When I returned home, Jacob proposed and I reluctantly said "no." If you'll remember, his flaw, in my mind, was his lack of ambition. My first love didn't have any dreams to see the world. He didn't want to don a cape and save that very world like I did. I didn't find him dynamic or animated or even passionate. Nevertheless, Jacob was a very good man. In fact, most women would see him as serious husband material. He really loved me, but didn't inspire me. I'd have to give up too much, as I imagined my radio career, the way I want to raise my children, and even the way and what I believed would be nothing but a clouded memory, never to emerge openly again, while Jacob worked at General Motors. I was reminded that this was not the life I wanted. He really was somebody else's dream man.

CHAPTER 2

MEETING STACEY

This is going to sound like a Lifetime Movie, but here goes. Between meeting Jacob and the eventual sociopath was Charles, my husband. I was married to Charles from 2005 to 2009. He is my daughter's father. You have lots of questions, I know. But don't get me started because all that will come of it is a fanciful journey into the unknown. I wanted to end it for a plethora of reasons, but suffice it to say, "I just felt like I should be married." To be married validated me, so I thought. I was "allowed" to be a mother as long as my daughter had a father. And Charles, well…he was around at the proverbial right time, despite not having any of the traits I wanted in a man. Rather, I was more impressed by the fact that his parents were together for some 30 years. I thought it was hereditary, I guess. In any event, it was clear that I was more married to the prospects of a long and loving institution instead of the raw reality that was facing me.

When I turned 26, I was divorced, and working at a radio station in the Midwest. I had just purchased my first home and was hoping to find a good relationship. Finding a good relationship? What did I know about a good relationship? Then there was a gnawing part of me that compelled me to ask myself over and over again "Why am I looking at all?" This question would eventually prove essential.

One night while out clubbing with friends, I was captivated by the skills of an amazingly talented DJ. Playing everything from reggae to house, he knew how to blend beats perfectly to keep people on the dance floor. As my friends and I lingered over drinks at the bar, I said, "Whoever the DJ is really knows how to rock a party." A friend answered, "That's DJ Spectrum." I'd heard of him and made a mental note to keep him in mind in case anyone asked me for a DJ recommendation. So, when my boss asked staffers about new DJs for our roster, I suggested that he get in touch with DJ Spectrum. Our station hired him. I worked from 2:00 p.m. to 6:00 p.m. during the week, and he mixed late nights on the weekend. Sometimes he would mix live, but usually he would simply turn in a CD to be played during his time slot. His real name was Stacey. He turned out to be one of the best DJs in the city. He was also incredibly handsome, anchored by his signature heart-melting smile. And he had a style to complement his youthful and creative spirit, including tight jeans, bright tees, and sneakers. One day he filled in for another DJ on my show. He showed up to mix that Tuesday afternoon with a beautiful girl he introduced as his girlfriend, Staci. I chuckled at the fact that both their names were pronounced the same way but had no time to continue the conversation. He went into a separate room to do the mix. After he was done, I did not see him for a long time. Also, I didn't think about the other Staci.

One day, I was sharing some thoughts about my own divorce with male colleagues. I was talking about how badly many men treat women. Stacey overheard me and barked, "The problem is you don't know what you want?" Defensively I responded, "Yes, I do and I won't settle." He continued the dialogue by asking, "What do you want then?" I thought, then said, "I want a man who is passionate about life, me, his career, his family, his community, and God." After a short pause I continued: "I want a man who will motivate me and inspire me. I want a man who will love the hell out of me!" He laughed. "Let's talk about this some more. What is your phone number?" I was puzzled, but succumbed to that smile. I gave him my number.

That night we stayed on the phone for four hours talking about everything from a book called *The Secret* to music, a source we both loved. We were also able to agree to disagree on many things. He said he believed that people could speak anything into existence. I told him that there are some things God just doesn't have for us. Our dialogue continued:

"I can talk about becoming a millionaire all day but I have to handle God's money well now."

"Or what?" he asked.

I responded, "Or he might not bless me with that financial expansion."

Maybe it was the substance in that dialogue or an internal feeling of optimism, but we grew closer and eventually started dating. No one had ever told me that a man could mistreat me without hitting me or sexually abusing me. In fact, I had never heard of emotional abuse and didn't know that there are many different ways for a man to beat up a woman without laying a hand on her or creating a single, visible bruise.

CHAPTER 3

THE GAMES BEGIN

In his classic, *Games People Play*, the late Dr. Eric Berne asserted that every relationship is a game. And why not? Everyone wants a successful relationship and if it requires a game to get it, then so be it. Winning, a necessary byproduct of a game, is sometimes fielded a little differently by women than men. I'm not saying this is a standard absolute, but it was true in my case. For me, winning is reaching a truthful outcome. Truth, to me, was exploring the measurable, tangible potential in the man. For many men, and certainly for the ones in my life, winning is all about getting what you want. I fought hard to win, at least as I saw winning. However, like so many of us, I focused on the potential, or on the "He could become *this* if I just give it time..." I never focused on what was truly there. And that was my loss. Literally!

The first time I went to Stacey's house it was around nine o'clock at night. I was worried because he lived in a less than desirable neighborhood.

Stacey's house, however, was new and modern and sleek, and very much out of place among the crack houses and alleyways. Inside, the house had cathedral ceilings, three bedrooms, wood floors, and a finished basement, with an area for him to blast music and practice mixing without disturbing anyone. If anyone ever told you to be suspicious in buying the best house in the worst neighborhood, then you can imagine my impressions of what I was seeing. Every portion of his house was a man cave, complete with countless shelves filled with records, three Apple computers housed in treasured cubicles, and pricey gadgets I couldn't even describe. All this stuff made the house cold. It wasn't a home. Homes are warm. This was definitely a house. A building. A dungeon.

Amidst all the gadgets, Stacey owned a comfortable sofa that he kept in that basement. I sat there for about an hour watching him put together a music mix for the station. He was in a zone, pausing only briefly to get me a cover, because he noticed I was chilly. Such a sweet gesture. So nurturing, so caring. I held on to those thoughts for as long as I could. Afterwards we talked for hours and listened to music until I finally looked up and saw it was 3:00 a.m. I told him I had to leave, but he wanted me to stay the night, adding that he would sleep in another room. I declined.

We walked up the stairs to the kitchen, but before I could reach the door, he gave me a passionate kiss. It was so unexpected. First kisses can be awkward, but for us there was an instant spark. I told him that I really had to leave, rushing for the door before I let my emotions get the better of me. The next day, Stacey called and asked me if I wanted to go to the mall. He knew that I needed to drop a pair of shoes off to get repaired, and suggested a place he knew that was close by. I picked him up and we stopped at the shop. He held my hand the entire time. I loved the sensation of his hand in mine, but I'm also a private person. I knew that the world of broadcasting was a very small world indeed and I didn't want rumors flying around about our romance—if it was a romance? I was nervous. Did I really want us to be viewed as an item?

We were careful in public but we still had fun. The consummate gentleman, he took me to new restaurants and was responsible for finding one of my favorite creole restaurants downtown. We went for walks, went to buy yogurt, looked at the stars. All our dates were simple, romantic and perfect. Because we were so connected I expected mind-blowing sex. Wrong! Our first time together was on that same old couch in his creepy, underground "man cave." A comfy couch, perhaps, but awkward sexual experience. I couldn't believe the utter lack of passion, given our first kiss. That kiss was flawless. We were united. We were one. I tried to think of reasons for his despondency. Stacey also shared his house with his brother Steve. Steve knocked on the door several times while we were exploring our first time together. Maybe he destroyed our vibe? Maybe Stacey was afraid of being interrupted? I was looking for an answer. Then I backed away from my own inquisition, because I was glad Stacey appeared to enjoy it. At least that is what I hoped. Even though I was disturbed. *Enjoyed it?* How about enjoyed me? Still, the innocent side of me just hoped it would be better next time.

In March, less than a month after we started dating, Stacey gave me a key to his house. He told me I could come over anytime and he really wanted me to have it. I tried to reject the offer because I felt like it was way too soon. But he insisted. A week later, I decided to surprise him and bring him dinner after I got off work. I stopped at his favorite noodle place and got his favorite dish. At about 6:30 p.m., I took my key, with dinner in hand, and walked into his house, the house in which I was welcome. The alarm went off. I tapped the code, shutting off the alarm, then turned and walked into his bedroom. He was asleep. The first thing I noticed was that the sheets were changed. The sheets that were on the bed the day before were now on the floor and a woman's white sweater laid on top of the pile. Then my heart dropped. I saw a pair of women's nude stilettos sitting on the wood bench at the end of his bed. I screamed, "OH SHIT!" Startled, he was awakened. As I stared at the shoes, I told him "I brought you dinner. I guess I will just leave it in the kitchen." He said, "Please don't leave." I ran into the kitchen, dropped the food on the counter and then rushed to the door with tears in my eyes. I left. The only problem was I forgot my laptop at his house and was forced to return. Before I went back to his house, I called my friend Kim. She worked at the radio station with me. Kim had gone to college with Stacey and had always spoken highly of him. She told me many times how she felt he was a total gentleman and very charming. I explained what had happened and she became livid. She said, "If you want, I can go there and get your things." I told her I would do it myself because I really wanted to see what he would say. So, I went back to his house.

I couldn't believe my ears when he uttered those first words:

"Do you want to handle this thing like an adult or keep acting like a child?"

I was speechless. Somehow he was placing the blame on me. He wasn't accountable. He felt blameless. He was just fine. I was the senseless one. I said, "Well let's hear what you have to say." He told me that his friend, Gina, was at his house the night before and had to work late. So, she changed clothes at his house and left her shoes. He even said, "We can call her and she will tell you." He continued to lie, even when claiming he would never lie to me. He added, "I know what you've been through and I would never hurt you." You have to learn to trust me." That was the moment I should have walked away. But I didn't. In hindsight, I wanted to believe him. After a failed marriage, I wanted to do things differently this time. I wanted to trust completely. I did, however, think that that Gina was someone who I would love to meet. After all, her incredible level of comfort around Stacey was admirable, right? Of course I'm sarcastic. It helped me live through the nightmare. I wanted to pretend the incident never happened. But that was impossible. *Stacey had potential.* I thought. Potential.

Acting on the "potential" of a person or situation as opposed to acting on what is right in front of your face requires that you to ignore reality completely. Seeing things that are not there. Internalizing a world that does not exist is what so many of us do. We want to be loved. We want to be respected. We cannot ignore our moral compasses, the one measure of sense and independence. Potential, our compass makes clear, is not headed in any direction. Potential forces us to meander from one point to another without any apparent destination. It only results in a toxic outcome.

CHAPTER 4

CRYING TIME

Who is this Gina lady? Why haven't I ever heard you speak of her? Why haven't I met someone yet who is cool enough to come over your house and change her clothes before work? What type of work does she do? Does she know about me?

Instead of asking Stacey those questions, I discussed the whole incident with my friend, Jasmine. I asked, "Do you know anyone named Gina that Stacey might know?" She said, "Yes! It must be the same Gina that is connected to some of Stacey's friends." Jasmine told me that the Gina she knew was a promotional model and went to the clubs at night to pass out samples of liquor and other items. After Jasmine described her to me, I knew exactly who she was. Gina was pretty, short, and curvy. She wore all kinds of wigs and weaves. Every time I saw her, I wasn't sure if it was her. She was constantly in disguise. I don't know if I was doing the right thing, but I asked Jasmine to call Gina and give her my phone number. She did.

I had just arrived to work when Gina called and we had the most curious conversation. I told her that I saw her shoes at Stacey's house but I was a little unsure of their relationship so I wanted to get things out in the open. Boy, did she ever. She told me that although she was Stacey's friend, it was a friendship with benefits. She admitted having a sexual relationship with Stacey.

Although it wasn't too surprising, I was still in shock. I hoped that somehow I was misconstruing the whole thing. I told her that I had a key to his house. Gina told me that she also had a key but was forced to give it back. She didn't explain the reason except that she was tired of his lies. I was pleased that our talk was civil and productive. There were no hard feelings between us and I ended the conversation with a simple, "Thanks for taking the time to talk to me."

I broke down in tears after I hung up the phone. I sent him a text about a half hour later. "I talked to Gina and I know everything." His response was, "I don't care." If learning that your boyfriend is a cheat isn't enough, just add in his ruthless lack of empathy, imposing more hurt that one can imagine. I did not respond to Stacey. I got smart, maybe for the first time in months. I realized that ignorance and dishonesty isn't worth my anger. This silent segment made an impression on him. I remember getting into my car and meeting up with my friends at the mall. The next thing you know it was text after text. My phone was blowing up with text messages from Stacey.

They read:

[I don't know what she said to you but she just doesn't want to see me happy.]

[Please call me.]

[I need to talk to you.]

[Why are you going to let this ruin what we have?]

Then, much like the second act of a play, the tone of the text messages changed.

[You want me to be miserable too!]

[You are just like Gina!]

[If you can't pick up the phone and call me then you don't care either.]

I finally decided to give the phone to my friends to read the rest of the messages and then delete them. I don't know why I wanted them to read the messages. I suppose I wanted evidence, some sort of reinforcing data pointing to his miserable, uncaring persona. Later that night, I convinced myself to call him.

The first thing I asked was, "Why would you cheat on me?"

He said, "I didn't cheat. You and I aren't together."

I was very confused. While we never said, "You and I are boyfriend and girlfriend," I thought the issuance of a key to his house was a strong signal, for goodness sake. "What do you mean we aren't together? You gave me a key to your place?" He said, "All my close friends have a key to my place." I was completely floored. He started to cry. Can you believe that? He started to cry. But here is something more confounding, even more unbelievable: After I hung up the phone, I was at his house comforting him.

Jay-Z came to town and Stacey hosted the after party when the concert was over. I stopped in and we talked for a bit and then he introduced me to the owner of the club.

"This is my girlfriend, JJ."

I can't deny it. I liked the way that sounded, despite the fact we still had never defined our relationship as such. Then, he gave me a kiss. "Pick me up when the party is over," he asked. I agreed, but when I showed up, he was not there. The only people left in the club were the cleaning crew. Then I received a text from Stacey. "I'm almost done, packing up." Another lie! But, if he wasn't in the club, where was he? It was a question that I never asked. I let that lie go. He came walking from around the corner with a big smile on his face and got into my car.

A few weeks later, a friend of mine asked, "I thought you were dating DJ Spectrum?"

"I am," I answered with some reluctance.

"Well, Tori's Facebook page is filled with photos of her and Spectrum at Jay-Z's after party. The captions read 'partying with my boo.'"

Tori was a popular club dancer in our city. She wasn't known so much for her great dance moves.

She was known for her butt. Every time someone mentions her name, it was followed by "that girl with the big ass." Stacey made it clear that this was one of the features that he loved most about Tori. When she wasn't dancing, Tori was a waitress at popular Mexican spot on the Westside.

I walked away without saying another word. I checked Tori's Facebook page and there was Stacey, hugging her. I wanted to confront him but knew it would lead to a nasty confrontation and I didn't want that.

A week later, he had a DJ'ing gig at the Zebra Lounge. I picked him up at 3:30 in the morning and drove him home. Fifteen minutes after we arrived, the doorbell started ringing and someone started banging on the front door. Next, I heard yelling. "Come to the door, dammit!" It was a woman and she was extremely upset. Stacey refused to get up until his brother Steve shouted at him, "Man, come handle this shit!"

He went outside to talk to the woman. I tried to listen at the window but I couldn't hear what either Stacey or the woman was saying. Furious, I went back to watching TV. Stacey returned twenty minutes later and begged me not to leave. He explained that the woman thought they were a couple and was upset when she saw us leaving the club together. He claimed that she had recently lost her grandfather and he had just helped her through a tough time.

The story sounded ridiculous. He saw suspicion on my face and began crying. Then, he became angry, like a spoiled little boy not getting his way, and threw a bottle of water at the wall. I had never saw this side of him. Did he regret hurting the girl's feelings? Was he embarrassed? I doubt it. I started to acknowledge Stacey as an emotionless creature capable of destroying anyone who gets in his way. I felt helpless and hopeless. My mind told me to get out of there. Instead, I did what he asked. I stayed. He stopped talking. He stared into space. He was still sitting there when I woke up hours later.

PART 2

HOW EMOTIONAL ABUSE WORKS

CHAPTER 5

MOM AND DAD

S tacey started spending hours sitting at his computer, looking up only to ask me to grab him something to eat. He would sometimes remain in the same spot for more than nine hours just staring at the screen. Yes, I thought this behavior was weird but I didn't want to cause problems, so I kept my mouth shut. I rationalized his behavior by thinking that everyone has an odd habit or two. He switched between Twitter and Evernote, surfing the web or searching through his archives of music while I napped and watched a lot of TV. He brought new meaning to the phrase "being in a zone."

The next woman was Briane. She worked for a marketing company in Milwaukee and had been helping Stacey get his mix tapes across the country with sponsors for a long time. He didn't hide his friendship with her. But, one day he needed me to print out a contract that she'd sent him. He forwarded her email to me.

"Have you found a girlfriend yet?" she asked.

"No. I'm waiting on you," he replied.

I shed a few tears and printed the contract. I took it to his house for him to sign, then took it to a local print shop in order to fax the signed copy back to her. All I thought about was how mad he would be when he saw that I had read through his email.

Looking back now, I realize that Stacey wasn't stupid. He wanted me to see it. I also know now that sociopaths will leave you signs to see how you will react.

In any case, back then I was devastated. By this time, my friends were tired of my Stacey stories and cries of "Leave him, Girl!" had become more frequent. In an ideal world, I would have been able to turn to my mother for advice but that wasn't possible.

I'm not sure what exactly sparked the evil in my mother's heart. No hugs, kisses or special moments of affection were shared between us, as I did with my dad. There was just this feeling of being terrified of her and her emotional cruelty.

I would get violent spankings for things like accidentally breaking a plate in the kitchen. My brother got beaten for filling up his glass to the brim with Kool-Aid, then not drinking it all.

It is clear now that my mother either had a severe mental illness or, at the very least, some type of emotional disorder. But a child believes that he or she creates crazed outbursts in adults. I was no different. I accepted every lash of her cruel words and swinging belt as punishments well deserved.

My parents divorced when I was nine. The cause was my father's cheating on her with another woman. One usually thinks of a divorce as a way to gain a sense of peace, loving yourself by gaining freedom from a relationship that is cutting you to pieces. But, once my dad left, my mother seemed to hurt even more, even though she had also cheated on him. The anger built up more and more.

One day after their final separation, my dad came to visit. He took me to eat at a cafeteria in the nearby mall. Not able to let us enjoy our time alone, my mother sought us out, stormed into the restaurant, grabbed Dad's glass of soda, threw it in his face and walked out.

I sat there crying as dad tried to calm me down. She was always doing stuff like that. Leading up to the end of their union, I vividly remember things like the day my mother threw all of dad's clothes on the front lawn when she found out he was cheating. I remember the day my father, who was a cop, took his gun out and walked down the middle of the street threatening to kill the man with whom she was cheating.

My father wasn't perfect, but at least he loved me. My mother, on the other hand, acted like she was possessed by a demon.

One day she came home from work, howling at the top of her lungs. I was in my room watching TV when the door flew open. She stood there with a belt in her hand. Her new boyfriend had told her that I called him an asshole, which was not true. What was true was that I didn't care for any of the men she brought home. I tried to convince her that he was lying but it was my word against his.

She would never have believed me anyway. My dad was gone, she and I were alone and the men in her life always came before me.

I was always a burden, blamed for her inability to find and keep a good man. Now, this latest piece of trash had lied on me. Filled with rage, she dragged me down to the basement and beat me until my legs and back had cuts all over them.

The next day, I told my dad what happened. He had some words with her boyfriend.

Months later, she finally broke up with the guy after he threw a log through our living room window. I overheard her telling one of her girlfriends on the phone that he was a liar. But she never apologized to me.

These scenes are carved into my memory, creating a negative inner story about who I was, what love was and who could possibly love me.

I never saw a successful, healthy relationship growing up.

CHAPTER 6

AND THE BEAT GOES ON

When someone is cheating on you, it hurts real bad. There is no woman, or man for that matter, who enjoys the feeling of being cheated on. Your stomach hurts, your head hurts, your heart aches and your thoughts go around in circles. *What did I do to cause this? What could I have done better?*

A million and one questions just like these flooded my mind. I obsessed over what those other women had that I didn't.

All I could think about was not being good enough. I never once thought, *I don't deserve to be treated this way.*

Then, like a small child who has gotten away with breaking too many rules, Stacey's behavior got much worse and it wasn't about cheating.

He started making me feel small. He told me I was worthless and dumb. He said I would look so much better with boob implants. My cooking wasn't up to par. I was unattractive and a horrible mom. Stacey said all of these things directly to my face but yet I still stayed around.

Late one night, I left my laptop charger at my house when I went over to visit Stacey. I asked to borrow one of his.

"You're stupid!" he shouted. "How could you forget your own charger?"

I began to cry. "Why is it such a big deal, Stacey? It was an accident. Besides, you have lots of chargers that I can use."

"Go home and get your own charger."

I went home and refused to come back. He called me so many times I lost count. Finally, I returned his call.

"What is it Stacey?"

"I don't like your Facebook profile picture. You need to change it."

"What?"

"Do it now," he ordered.

I changed it immediately. Not long after that, I slowly began to change. I accepted every comment, demand and criticism of me.

I made every change that he asked for to keep him happy.

One day, while sitting on the couch. He sat down next to me and I laid my head on his shoulder as we watched TV.

He looked at me and said, "You're lucky to be with me, Jillian." I raised my head up and he looked directly into my eyes. "You didn't finish college, you have a kid and you've been married and divorced. I'm telling you, you better watch your step because you are damn lucky to have me."

I cried until I ran out of tears then left his house and refused to take his calls.

A day later, he took a train to Milwaukee to see Briane. We didn't talk the entire weekend.

I saw pictures of a hotel room on his Facebook page. It was beautiful and it obviously cost a lot of money to stay there. When he returned, he admitted to spending the entire weekend with her and blamed me for pushing him away with my attitude.

Before I could get over this turn of events, another woman came into the picture.

A week after his Milwaukee trip, we attended an event at a jazz club. We went up to the bar to get some drinks. This is where I first laid eyes on Camille. She had a very light complexion with a hooked nose similar to the Wicked Witch of the West, gorgeous green eyes and a quiet demeanor. She was at the bar, too. She and Stacey didn't speak to each other but I sensed that they knew each other. I could just feel it.

Later on, I left Stacey to greet some friends. When I turned to look back, Stacey and Camille were engrossed in conversation.

After that night, whenever Stacey DJ'ed at a club, Camille was in the audience. EVERY SINGLE TIME. One night, Camille introduced me to the man she was with.

Afterwards, I told Stacey: "I met your friend, Camille and her boyfriend. They seem nice."

He responded, "Long story about her and

Mike."

Mike was Stacey's best friend.

"Tell me."

"Well, she and Mike once had a fling. She was married at the time. Her husband found out about it while reading her diary, and blew his lid. He even contacted Mike's wife and told her about the affair. All hell broke loose. Camille and her husband got divorced."

"When I first saw her, I thought something might be going on between the two of you."

Stacey replied, "We did at some point."

"You had sex with her?"

"Yeah."

"Before or after your best friend was involved with her?"

I knew that I should have stopped asking questions before things got any worse but I continued. "So, you had sex with a woman who contributed to the destruction of your best friend's marriage. Who does that?"

He immediately snapped. "Who are you to be judgmental? You don't know the situation. It wasn't that serious."

I thought to myself, it wasn't that serious but it was serious enough that the woman's husband divorced her. Now his best friend's wife no longer trusts him. Sounds pretty serious to me.

Of all the women to date or have sex with my best friend's fling wouldn't be on the list.

I wish I could say that Camille eventually went away but she didn't.

It was Thursday night, Stacey was DJ'ing an event that was right across the street from an event I was hosting. After my hosting duties were complete, I went across the street to visit him. I sat down in the DJ booth next to Mike. Camille appeared and she gave Stacey a hug. She said hello to Mike and he looked away.

She walked up closer to him. "You still aren't going to talk to me after all this time?"

"Hi, Camille."

She gave him a hug and walked out.

Mike looked at me and I shook my head about the situation between them.

"Do you know what happened?" he asked.

I denied knowing the details. "I just don't understand why she won't speak to me. She knows that I'm Stacey's girlfriend."

Mike replied, "She has issues. Don't pay her any mind."

A few days later, I asked Stacey to take me to get my hair done at the salon. He dropped me off around 12 noon. He insisted on going inside to meet my stylist. I wasn't sure if it was his insecurity or just a way to make sure he was a part of everything I did. When he left the salon, he took my car.

When he returned three hours later, he complimented my hair and how good I looked. But, when I opened the passenger door of my car, I noticed an unfamiliar shirt in the back seat. It was a woman's medium and dark blue.

"Stacey, whose shirt is this in the back of my car?" I asked.

"I don't know, maybe it's my brother's."

"What do you mean, MAYBE it's your brother's shirt? It wasn't here when you dropped me off."

The shirt said Northwest University on it. I remembered one of my friends telling me that Camille was in one of her classes at Northwest. "Why don't you know whose shirt this is?"

He flipped the script. "Stop accusing me of something I didn't do," he screamed. "Why are you talking to me in such a foul and aggressive manner?"

I just stood there.

"You are disrespectful and do not know how to talk to a man!"

With that, he ended the conversation. I never found out whose shirt was in my car. All I could do was assume it was Camille's. But, he definitely had been with someone while I was having my hair done. Most likely, he had sex in the car.

That night, I stayed at his house and, when I asked him for a shirt to sleep in, he handed me the shirt from my car.

My friends were tired of being angry with

Stacey, comforting me, worrying about me and trying to figure out how to help me when I refused to help myself.

Everyday a part of me was washed away, never to be found. I didn't even realize that it was happening. I accepted being treated like a dog. A woman in her normal mind would have been on the first train coming to get away from the drama. I started feeling crazy.

A few days later, I tried to log in to my laptop but my laptop would not accept my password. I called Stacey from work and told him something was wrong with my laptop. He asked me if I tried to turn it off and turn it back on. Of course I did.

"I can't log in because it's saying that it's not the correct password."

He asked me if I had tried other passwords. Maybe I had forgotten it. My password had been the same for years. I obviously knew my password.

"You were the last person to use my laptop today." I told him.

He yelled at me for accusing him of messing up my laptop. I listened to him scold me for about 10 minutes before I started crying. He suggested I try using a different password.

"Use *I love Stacey*," he said.

I typed it in and it worked. My laptop password had always been "I love my baby girl." I could not understand how or why he did it, or why he would make me feel like I was the one that was stupid for not being able to figure out how to log into my own laptop.

"Why would you do this?" I asked.

"I don't have time to talk. You've wasted enough of my time," he replied.

He hung up quickly. Mind game after mind game, day after day. It became my norm. I was constantly trying to figure out things that I could never understand. Why would he put me through these mind games? What did I do to deserve this? I continued to put up with the games. I allowed myself to enter into his world of chaos and I remained there suffering until I couldn't take anymore. Stacey would say the most shocking things when we would have arguments; anything to take the heat off of him. He told me once that if

I really truly loved him, I would have introduced him to my daughter.

"How can you love me when you are keeping the most important parts of you away from me?" He told me.

I actually agreed with him. I made the worst mistake and made my daughter a part of his crazy world. Two days later I took her over to his house to meet him. He seemed to be excited but behind that smile was something not so authentic. I felt it. Stacey never liked kids. He always spoke badly about his own nephews. Most of the time, when my daughter would came over he would go into his dungeon basement and never even show his face. Stacey didn't seem like a "kid friendly" type of guy. It was something I should have considered before assuming he was the man of my dreams.

Stacey tended to overreact to things. I once overheard Stacey on the phone with a promoter telling him he was not going to DJ a party because his name wasn't big enough on the flyer. He once made a mix CD for an up and coming artist living in LA. It took him about a full week of working nonstop to put it together. He completed it and turned it in. A few days later the artist responds to Stacey and thanks him.

"Thank you. Good work."

The next thing I knew, Stacey is sitting in front of his laptop in tears. Then he starts going into a rage throwing things everywhere. Scared for my life, I asked what was wrong.

"All this guy said was, "Thank you. Good work," he replied.

He went into emotional rages from time to time that left me afraid. He pushed me up against the wall one day but never hit me. I always thought the time would come. There was nothing consistent with his behavior. He was always irrational.

One of the scariest feelings to have is the feeling of losing control. I did whatever he told me to do and no longer recognized the person in the mirror. I became the person Stacey wanted me to be. My friends noticed the change but they couldn't get me to listen. Time after time my friends begged me to leave him. They even tried to put together an intervention. It could never have happened though because he wouldn't let me spend time with my friends. I didn't even spend time with my own child. My daughter was always with a friend.

Stacey became my life. He was my top priority.

My guy friends just believed Stacey was a player.

I now realize that they were wrong. There was something seriously wrong with Stacey in the psychological sense. He was unable to exhibit compassion or to feel remorse. He enjoyed inflicting emotional pain and there was nothing I could have done to fix the situation.

Stacey needed psychiatric help.

CHAPTER 7

ROCK BOTTOM

I changed the way I thought. I'm sure it was my self-esteem telling me that I could not do better. I had totally convinced myself that with all the drama going on, he was still the most incredible person on earth. He was the one I would spend my life with. There wasn't a man out there that was as great as him. I was fooling myself. Living in this place, far from reality, was a scary place to be. I had lost all control. I had lost all common sense. I had lost me.

It was May and time for the Kentucky Derby; a big deal in the Midwest during that time. Stacey was asked to DJ a party by a promoter. He accepted the offer and asked me if I would take him there and spend the weekend. Stacey didn't have a car. I thought it was pretty odd that someone who made good money in the club every week didn't have a car to drive. He drove his brother's brand new black Jeep at times. But the majority of the time, he was driving my car. There was a car that sat in his garage I asked him about. It was an older model blue Honda Civic. He told me this long story about how he lost the key to the car and that it was over $800 to make a new one. I didn't have experience with getting new keys made for a car but it seemed like an outrageous amount of money. Even still, he could afford to do it. Two of the tires were flat. I asked him how long the car had been sitting there and he said since January; almost five months unused. Once again, the story sounded a little odd but I went along with it.

One day I went over to his house and his mom and stepdad were pushing the car out of the driveway. They said someone was coming to tow the car over to their house. Still, I asked no questions. Come to find out it was his parents car after all. I find it interesting that Stacey was consistently attacking parts of my life when he couldn't even maintain something as small as a vehicle given his level of success.

The time came to go to Louisville for the Kentucky Derby. I packed our stuff into my SUV and we hit the road. Once we arrived, there wasn't time to do anything; he had to go set up. I dropped him off at the party and came back later. When I walked into the party I saw him staring at a girl and she was staring back smiling. I've never been the possessive type or even confrontational, I just laughed and walked up to the DJ booth and waved. He seemed caught off guard but yet continued to work. After the party, we went back to the hotel and he said he wanted to smoke outside for a bit. A bit turned into almost two hours. I remember waking up and looking at the clock looking for him. I called his phone. No answer. He sent me a text.

[I'll be there in a sec]

I could feel something wasn't right. I wasn't sure if he was outside with another woman or just on the phone with one but my instincts assured me that another woman was involved somehow. This happened more than a few times over the course of our relationship. I eventually found out the truth about that night and it didn't surprise me one bit. It seemed he just could not be faithful. No matter how hard I tried to be the best girlfriend, he would still cheat.

There were times when I would get dressed to go out to the club with him and he would look at me and just say, "You look trashy," and walk out and leave in my car. He also controlled how I wore my makeup. He would tell me "Stop wearing eyeliner on the top of your lids. You need to wear it under your eye too. How you wear it now looks ugly." It started to remind me of when my mom used to tell me not to leave the house without lip gloss on. "You aren't going to put ANY lip gloss on?" I was never good enough.

He also didn't like me spending time with my friends who I missed so much. It seemed to me that they were drifting away. I couldn't remember the last time I had spent some fun time with them individually or as a group.

So, I called some of my friends and suggested that we go to a casino. Everyone was on board but, when I told Stacey, he shot the plan down.

"No I really want you to stay here. I need to use your car tonight."

He claimed he wanted me to be there when he got back home and even suggested I should take a bath and watch a movie. Do the things that I enjoy doing. So I didn't go. Instead I sat at his house. I felt sad and lonely. Most importantly, I felt hurt by the fact that I had disappointed my friends. I believe he enjoyed keeping me away from my friends. Stacey did not want me to be happy. He wanted total control over everything I did.

Everyone knew that Stacey had inappropriate relationships with other women. The rapper, Common, came to town on a Thursday night. Stacey told me that he and his best friend, Mike, were going to the show. Since I had just seen Common a few months before, I opted out of going to the show. The day of the show came and Stacey said Mike couldn't go so he was going by himself. He took my car without even asking and went to the concert. The next day my boss told me he saw Stacey at the Common show. I was confused because I wasn't sure why he was even telling me. Then he told me he saw him driving my car. He didn't say anything else but I couldn't help but feel he wanted to say more.

I walked into the studio to do my show.

"Who was the girl Stacey was with last night at the concert?" one of my co-workers asked bluntly.

At that point Stacey and I were finally in a good place so I was shocked. Questions darted through my mind. He couldn't have picked up a date IN MY CAR and took someone to the concert!

"He went by himself so I'm sure that it was just one of his female friends that he saw there," I replied.

"Nope. They walked in together. You know you can do better than him," he quickly shot back and walked away.

Of course, Stacey denied everything and became angry when I tried to get the truth out of him. We were in a predictable, destructive pattern at this point. He cheated or hurt me in another way. I cried. I got myself over it. He cheated or hurt me again. I cried. I got myself over it, etc.

I had heard Stacey talk about Carmen a few times. I don't know where they met or how. She was short and chubby. She wore her hair very short like the '95 version of Toni Braxton. She was a regular girl who may not have turned the heads of anyone else but she certainly caught Stacey's attention. He told me she had a daughter that was mentally challenged. He made me feel like their friendship was strictly platonic. I should have known better. I remembered he told me some stranger tried to break into her home while she was there. She called Stacey since he lived only a few blocks away and he stayed the night with her just to calm her nerves. I believed him. The way he told the story seemed realistic. So I stayed at his house and he stayed at hers.

One weekend Stacey and I got into an argument over a pair of panties I found under his bed. I left his house outraged on a Saturday evening and didn't talk to him until Monday morning. He sent me a text:

[I miss you]

I knew immediately he had done something wrong. I called him and asked him what he did Sunday.

"I went to IKEA with Carmen," he said.

"And did you sleep with her?"

"Yes," he replied.

I was beginning to see a pattern; any woman remotely close to Stacey he probably slept with her. Never have I checked my boyfriend's cell phone until I met Stacey. I just had to know.

Several times in the middle of the night, I would wake up and go to the basement where his phone would be charging and I would check his text messages. I would see text messages from lots of other women. Most had fake names and it was so obvious that "Troy" was really "Tori" just by what they mentioned in the conversation. She texted:

[What club are you working at tonight?]

[Don't you want to rub on my booty?]

The text was a dead giveaway. I did notice another text message from a woman who was asking him to open the garage and she said she was at his house. I saw the date of the text matched with the weekend I was out of town visiting family. It was my life. Anytime I was gone with my daughter or the few times that he allowed me to go out with my friends, he was always with another woman.

The embarrassment really started to kick in. We were both in the public eye; everyone paid attention. Stacey was flaunting girls all around the city and most of the time I was clueless. After work I went to his house to finish washing his clothes. It wasn't uncommon for me to go through his pockets to empty out things in order to wash clothes. I took the pants he wore the night before and saw two torn ticket stubs for the concert. I went to put the pants in the washing machine and casually asked Stacey, "Who did you go to that concert with that night?"

He said, "No one. Why are you asking me this when I already told you that Mike couldn't go? He was getting defensive and angry.

"Well, I just pulled these two torn tickets out of your pocket," I replied.

He claimed the people just tore both tickets because he handed them two tickets. I dropped the conversation and continued to wash clothes. It wasn't like I believed him. I knew Stacey was a liar. He lied all the time. I just didn't seem to care anymore. It was clear that my self-esteem was shot. I didn't deserve to be involved with a man that treated me so poorly. But I am the one who chose to stay. Week after week, drama kept popping up but I just became accustomed to it.

One day, while at his house, he asked me if I could help to clean up. I agreed to help organize some things while he was at work. I wanted to do nice things for him. What he wanted me to do was completely outrageous but at the time I was willing to do anything to make him happy and to feel loved. He asked me to take all of his t-shirts (about 300 of them) and iron them and neatly fold them using the folding board similar to those you see employees using in department stores. He also asked for me to clean the bedroom and bathroom, so I got started. There was no doubt that this would take me a few days to complete. I started off cleaning his bedroom, then cleaned his bathroom then I started taking the shirts, one by one, ironing and folding them. While in his closet I decided to straighten up and create a more organized system for his clothes. I picked up his travel bag and decided to clean it out along with his two suitcases. Little did I know what I would find inside the bag. I found two empty condom wrappers and a pair of black thong panties. Stacey and I had just returned from our Louisville trip. At first, I thought the panties were mine. I was devastated. I was so angry and furious. Even more so, I could not leave his house to go home because Stacey had my car. So I called my friend Jasmine and begged her to come pick me up and take me to get my car. What a night.

Jasmine came to his house to pick me up and took me to the club where he was spinning that night. I asked her to wait outside while I went inside to ask for my car keys. With the travel bag in hand, I walked into the club with sweat pants and a t-shirt on. The club was packed. I walked into the DJ booth.

"Where is my car?" I demanded.

"What is this about? What is wrong?"

"I just need to know where my car is, Stacey." I replied calmly.

I never raised my voice or made a scene. I had a reputation to keep. I was already looking crazy by walking into the club with the attire I had on so I just wanted the process to be quick and easy so I could leave.

"Please tell me what this is about."

I handed him the travel bag. He opened it up and saw the black thongs. He immediately shut it and put under the table with his book bag.

"Where are my keys?" I asked again.

"We must talk about this; please don't do this

right now," he replied.

I asked him for my keys a few more times and then finally after going through his things, I got my keys. He asked me to please stay and talk to him. But I couldn't stay.

I asked him to tell me where he parked my car and I left the club. I went to a 24-hour breakfast restaurant up the street from the club with my friend and just cried and cried. What amazed me was that even when things like this happened and Stacey was so wrong, I still thought about his feelings.

After wiping the tears away, I couldn't help but wonder how he was going to get home. The thought of him having to call another girl to take him home made me angrier. I still felt sad for him, no matter how bad the pain. While he was DJ'ing, he sent me multiple messages that turned from him pleading to being violent.

[Why are you going through my things in the first place?]

[You are so insecure!!!]

[I've seen some of your ex-husband's things at your

house, but I never freaked out on you!]

It stunned me how he could even come up with that comparison. He saw a pair of my ex-husband's sneakers in the garage that I was putting out for a yard sale. I mean, he did used to live at the house for years. He was my ex-husband. Finding a worn thong and empty condom wrappers in a travel bag that had to be used recently was not the same thing. The next morning, very early, I went to his house to get the rest of my things. He was asleep. I was expecting to see a woman at the house but there was no one else there. He made me feel like I was totally out of order. He made me feel like I was scum. Like always, I was to blame for what happened. This was our vicious cycle. Whenever he got caught, he would reverse it to make it about me. And the women kept piling up.

Then there was Danielle. All I knew of Danielle was that she worked at the door of a club that I hosted on Sunday nights. We would speak briefly as I entered the door. She and I never had much conversation. We would occasionally talk about how long the line was or something I may have said on my show. She was very friendly. She was very good friends with Camille too. I saw them together often. She was brown-skinned with Asian-looking eyes. She favored Erykah Badu to me. She wore her hair very short with a natural curl. She dressed like a tomboy. One of Stacey's ex-girlfriends told me it was no secret that Stacey had a threesome with Camille and Danielle. Once I found out, I never spoke to her again. See, this is what we do as ladies, especially when our heads are screwed up. We decide to have an issue with the OTHER woman (or women in this case), rather than having an issue with the common denominator, the Man. I saw Danielle speaking to Stacey in the club. I remember her being overly nice once when she saw me in the DJ booth. She came up and gave me a hug. She told me how cute Stacey and I looked together. Stacey just seemed to ignore her while he was working; her tone just seemed a little sarcastic. I felt like I needed to keep a watch on her.

The last of the seven women I knew about was Necole. I walked in on Stacey on the phone speaking with a woman. He was blushing like a little schoolgirl while talking to her. He was saying that he was going to be in California and that he would love to see her. Naturally, I didn't think it was anyone he was interested in because he clearly saw me sitting there while he conversed with her on the phone. He told me that she was his best friend's ex-girlfriend and that she lived in California. He just wanted to catch up with her. He talked about how in love his BFF was with this woman when they were in college but they just didn't work out. I couldn't help but think how interesting it was that Stacey managed to stay in contact with the lovers of his best friend. Seemed a little unusual to me but hey...everything about him was unusual. Time passed and I didn't hear anything else about Necole until one night I went over to Stacey's house and he had fallen asleep in front of his computer. Up on the screen in front of him was a chat session with Necole. They shared a pretty intense sexual conversation including what he would like to do to her and in return she shared a few half-naked pictures of herself. Nowhere in the conversation did he ever mention he had a girlfriend.

Stacey was beyond just a player. I've been played before in the past. Most of the player types are very slick and smart about how they cheat. Stacey left way too much evidence. It was like he did it on purpose. Who would do such things? I did nothing but try to love Stacey exactly how he wanted to be loved. I sacrificed my time for him, even the time with my four-year-old daughter and my friends just to make him happy. I was never good enough. No matter what I did, he always ran into the arms of another woman. No matter how hard I tried, he always made me feel like I was nothing.

Even with people seeing me cry almost every day at work, no one could understand what was going on. No one could see how my mind was being twisted into knots daily. I imagine from the outside looking in, it probably just seemed like a bad relationship. It was much more than that. I just wanted to fix it. So I felt the need to dig a little deeper. I went to Stacey's house one Saturday afternoon and didn't hear a sound in the house. I went downstairs to his basement and there he sat with his head down in front of his computer, but this time he was crying. I asked what was wrong and he handed me a letter that had come in the mail. The letter said that his house was in foreclosure. There were other people's names on the letter so I was slightly confused and then he explained.

The owners of the house were renting the house to Stacey. All this time Stacey said he had bought this lavish house but he didn't. The actual owners foreclosed on the house and told him that it's only a matter of time before the bank kicked him out. Until then, the owners allowed him to remain there rent-free. I suggested to Stacey that he just buy the house. He told me that his credit was not in good standing because of credit card debt. He had an outstanding Discovery Card bill for $2,000. Stacey could have easily paid that off. He had the money. He also opened up about his driver's license being taken away for unpaid tickets. Then he starts pouring out information that had nothing to do with what we were talking about.

He kept crying and talking about his father leaving him and how he didn't want anything to do with him. I've never heard Stacey talk about his father. I've asked about him in the past but he just told me that he lives in Kansas.

He continued to tell me that he just talked to his father that same day and his dad asked him why he kept calling him. It was hard for me to imagine a parent saying this to his own child but by the look in Stacey's teary eyes this must have crushed him. I tried to believe what Stacey was saying but it seemed so exaggerated. I spoke to his father once. Later in the relationship, Stacey called me crying and I couldn't' even understand what he was saying. He hung up and I tried continuously to call back but no answer. Then I received a text that said to call his dad and he sent me the number. I wasn't sure what I was supposed to say to his dad. I didn't know if this was the reason why he was crying. But I called.

He answered the phone. Stacey told me his dad had very long dreadlocks so I put together a mental picture of the man I thought was on the other end of the phone.

"Hello, this is Stacey's girlfriend. He told me to call you."

He took a long sigh and arrogantly replied, "Hi, what is wrong THIS time?"

I told him about Stacey's crying spells and how I've seen him do this over and over. He spoke very intelligently. As he should, being that he is a judge.

"What did Stacey tell you is wrong with him?" He asked.

"I don't know. But he seems bipolar. One minute he is fine and smiling from ear to ear and then the next minute he is crying waterfalls."

"Is that what Stacey told you? Did he say he was bipolar?"

When he asked that question I immediately felt like he wanted to say something but couldn't. I told him that Stacey says he gets depressed sometimes because of how people treat him.

He sighed again and said, "I'll try to call Stacey. Thanks for calling me."

That was it. I never heard from him again nor did Stacey ever mention his name again. The search for answers continued. My gut told me that people knew more than what they were saying.

CHAPTER 8

WHEN WORSE GOT WORSE

I know it was really difficult for people to understand that all these things were going on in my life. From the outside looking in, you saw a successful woman. It looked like I was living the good life. I didn't discuss a lot of things that were going on with other people because I didn't want to hear them speak badly about Stacey. I knew they couldn't really understand. I was in the deepest hole and no one's arms were long enough to pull me out. I just kept sinking and sinking. When I look back now at some of the situations that happened that year, I still weep. I feel bad for the old me. I feel even worse for the women that I know are going through these things and have no idea what is going on.

Some weeks had passed and Stacey said he was going to take me on a date. We were sitting in this beautiful Italian restaurant downtown that wasn't too far from his house. We were having a delicious meal and enjoying the night.

Out of nowhere, Stacey said, "I bet you've always wondered about the women that I have been cheating on you with."

I gave him a disturbed look.

He continued, "Well, I know it crossed your mind to know what it's like for me to have sex with these women. I'll tell you."

He proceeded to tell me, one by one, what it was like to have sex with each one of the seven girls he cheated on me with. He told me that it was hard to have sex with Carmen because he wasn't physically attracted to her at all.

Gina, he said was boring and she would just lay there and didn't move. He said Necole was okay and so was Tori but he mostly just enjoyed her body and oral sex. He said that he did enjoy sex with me and that I was the best person he had sex with next to Camille. As a matter of fact, his exact words about this woman was, "Camille can squirt. If you could squirt, you would be much better than Camille in bed."

After that conversation, I sat there for a moment just frozen. My eyes were full of tears. I couldn't even believe that this happened. I couldn't believe the words that were coming out of his mouth. After dinner, he smiled as the waiter walked up to the table, he asked me to pay the check and we walked to my car. He got into the driver's seat and we drove back to his place. Neither of us spoke a word. I just cried all the way back home. Once I arrived back at his house, I cried myself to sleep like I had done numerous times during our relationship.

I couldn't do anything right. On my mission to please him and put a smile on his face, I would try to do what I thought a woman should do. I kept his house clean but it never met his standards. I would clean his bathroom and he would come right into the bathroom, snatch the cleanser and sponge from my hands and redo everything. "What DO you know how to do? Do you think someone is going to marry you again and you can't even clean?" There were a few times that I would make the bed and he would immediately pull off all the sheets off and say, "Start over." He would show me how he liked the sheets on the bed to look and then take the sheets right off and have me do it until I got it right.

I decided I needed to take a solo trip. I made it a routine to visit Miami at least once a year, so I decided that would be my getaway. I couldn't wait to relax on the beach. It was a well-deserved trip. Stacey had so many questions when I told him I was going to Miami alone.

Who are you staying with? What hotel? Why are you going alone? It was like he was paranoid. He was going to be in San Diego during that time working a gig. I was originally supposed to accompany him on this trip. I later found out he was also supposed to take his ex-girlfriend Staci. I booked my ticket to Miami, and as it got closer to the date that he was supposed to depart, I checked his phone to look through his text messages. I found a text to a woman name Shelly. He was encouraging her to come to the party where he was DJ'ing at in San Diego. I never mentioned it.

He flew out to San Diego on a Thursday. I flew out to Miami on that Saturday. Thursday night he called me and told me that he was going to sleep early. I thought it was awkward, since he is such a night owl but as always I gave him the benefit of the doubt. I figured he was probably tired from the flight and hanging out with his boys all day.

Saturday I arrived in Miami and he told me and he had a surprise for me. He told me he would be coming to Miami to see me. He knew this was my time to be away to relax and I made clear that I really wanted to be alone. He didn't care. It was always about what Stacey wanted. Saturday, I enjoyed sitting on the beach, checking out the local restaurants and enjoying my time alone. The next day Stacey arrived at my hotel; I was actually happy to see him. As soon as we got to the hotel room he told me how much he missed me. We had passionate sex before heading out to the beach. We stayed out on the beach for a while, and then we grabbed a bite to eat. While walking back to the hotel, we passed a local tattoo shop and went inside.

Stacey had been pressuring me for quite some time to get a tattoo to cover some of my Vitiligo patches. He hated the white spots on my body and had no problem telling me how they were ugly and I should keep them covered up at all times. I found an article one day online that recommended people with Vitiligo stay away from eating eggs and citrus. I shared what I had learned with Stacey but his response caught me off guard. Starting the very next day, he made me scrambled eggs, cream of wheat and a glass of orange juice for breakfast. He would have it so neatly displayed on the kitchen table with the finest plates in the house and a small flower in a teacup as a centerpiece. Every time I would spend the night at his house he would cook the same thing for breakfast. I expressed to him the very first time that I couldn't eat it because I was trying to help my skin to heal from this skin condition. He called me ungrateful. He yelled at me and expressed his hurt that I wouldn't eat the food that he unselfishly prepared for me. So I ate it. I ate it every time.

I felt like it was mean that he would even suggest that I cover up my Vitiligo spots with tattoos but my low self-esteem gave in to his request and I got the tattoo that day. He already had the design in mind. He picked out a red star that covered a spot on my wrist. The next day while Stacey was in the shower, I looked over and saw his phone on the bed. I shook my head and tried my best to talk myself out of going through his phone. By now, I would expect to find something inappropriate in his phone. I picked up the phone only to find a text to a girl requesting her to come back to his hotel room the Friday night before. He did everything but beg her. The girl never responded or maybe he deleted her responses. I don't know. I saw another text he sent to Shelly asking if she was still going to try to make it to the party he was DJ'ing and how much he couldn't wait to see her.

I heard Stacey turn off the shower and I quickly put his phone back on the bed. The problem came when I didn't set his phone back to the original screen. Once he got out the shower he noticed my attitude had changed and immediately looked at his phone. He picked it up and then looked at me.

"Oh, so you are still doing this? What do you want to know? I can just tell you," he said sarcastically.

"Why are you still cheating?"

He yelled, "I'm not cheating! What makes you think that?"

"You have asked two women in one day to come see you. I don't know either of these women."

He told me one was a friend from college and one was just a woman he met that wants him to DJ an event.

"Look! I have her card!"

"Yeah, but why are you asking her to come to your hotel at 4:00 a.m. in the morning, Stacey?"

"I really just wanted to talk to her."

"Riiiiight," I responded.

I was absolutely pissed at this point. He went into a rage about me going through his phone and how we have worked so hard to build trust back up but me going through his phone has destroyed what we had. He said he could never trust me again. I left the hotel in tears. We flew out at two totally different times. I thanked God I didn't have to ride back with him on the airplane. I took the time while on the flight to think about my life with Stacey. I tried to think of all of the positive things in our relationship. I started to think about the time that Stacey came over and cleaned my garage. It took him seven hours. He built shelves and hug ladders on the wall. He swept and everything. It looked immaculate once it was completed. I had such a great feeling of joy that day. Just him cleaning my garage made me feel special. The only problem was every great gesture was followed by a ton of self-esteem stompers. Stacey was good for making me feel good and then breaking me completely down. The bad definitely outweighed the good. My friends begged me to leave Stacey alone; I just couldn't see what they saw.

I returned home from Miami and everything went back to normal. It was our routine. We fought and then we acted like nothing happened. One day, Stacey and I went to my hometown on a Saturday afternoon to go shopping. While there, we stopped to see my brother and sister-in-law. We got into an interesting conversation about relationships and how to make them work. My brother talked about communication and keeping God first. Stacey never shared his spiritual views with me. For some reason, I never asked. What used to be a top priority to me had changed. I do remember him telling me how he attended the mosque a while back. He studied the Koran and was active in the Nation of Islam. We never had any spiritual conversations although I was a very spiritual person. Well, I was before meeting Stacey. There were so many signs that I was losing myself. I was slowly deteriorating.

When we left my brother's house and got into the car, Stacey said, "I don't think your brother is as smart as he appears to be."

I didn't know what to say. "Where did that come from? " I asked.

"I'm just making an observation; you don't need to get upset. It's my opinion."

I didn't say a word. We had one more stop before heading back home. It was time for my father to meet my boyfriend. My dad had met most of the guys that I had been in relationships with, from my first real boyfriend, Jacob who he really liked, to my ex-husband who he didn't feel deserved me. My father never offered his opinion much about the men I dated. He may jokingly say, "That young fella is weird," or "You need some new eyeglasses, Baby?" But my dad would always talk about Jacob. He knew that he was a hard worker plus they had so much in common. They both loved fishing! I believe that deep down my dad was disappointed that it never worked between us, even though he would never say it.

Stacey and I pulled up to my dad's house. I had to try and fix my attitude because I was still upset about Stacey's negative words about my brother.

The door opened and my dad gave me a big hug and kiss. "Well, this must be Stacey."

Stacey immediately turned on the charm. He asked my dad about being on the police force and what he thought about the relationship between the police and the community. My dad wouldn't look at Stacey, which really bothered me. It wasn't like him at all. I felt like my dad was being rude. We had a long drive ahead of us so I told my dad that we needed to get on the road. As soon as we got on the road, Stacey fell asleep and I felt it was the perfect time to call my dad. I called him and asked what he thought of Stacey.

"I don't have to like him honey. I just need to know that he treats you right, " he responded.

CHAPTER 9

HE ISN'T ALONE

They say birds of a feather flock together. I had always believed that Stacey's best friend was a cheater. I overheard many conversations and saw many text messages where they rooted each other on for their inappropriate ways. It was disgusting. But that wasn't the only person that had something in common with Stacey. There were rumors of his family having a history of mental illness. Rather than seeing this as a sign to walk away, I saw it as a cry for help. I felt as if I had to save Stacey, when I really should have been trying to save myself.

Stacey's younger brother Steve lived with him for a few years. He was twenty-six years old and very handsome. He was a biology teacher at one of the local colleges in the city. I had only seen him in passing a few times. He never went into Stacey's part of the basement unless he had to wash clothes. One day I was in the bedroom talking to my best friend on the phone and I walked into the living room to see Steve staring at a wall. His eyes were bloodshot red and it looked as if he were crying. I hung up with my best friend and asked him if he was okay. Continuing to glare at the wall, he didn't answer me. I ran downstairs and told Stacey something was wrong with his brother and he needed help. Stacey didn't budge. He simply pulled up an article about Schizophrenia on his computer. He got out of his chair, told me to sit down and read the article. I read it and questioned if he was trying to tell me that his brother was schizophrenic.

In the meantime, I started to panic because Stacey had still not gone upstairs to check on his brother. He called his mother and talked to his mother who assured him that Steve was okay. In my eyes, Steve was not okay. Days after that awkward situation, I saw Steve staring at the TV when I came over to Stacey's one Saturday morning; the TV was not on. He sat staring at a blank screen. I said hello but he didn't say a word. Rarely would he talk or even acknowledge that I was there, Stacey didn't even speak to him. I remember having nightmares all the time while spending the night over Stacey's house and it was always a dream about his brother going crazy and trying to hurt me. A few hours later, I came upstairs to get something to drink and he was still sitting in front of the TV. Stacey never mentioned it so I didn't say anything either, although it really creeped me out. Stacey and I left that afternoon and returned about 8:00 PM that night. Steve was sitting in the same spot starting at the TV. Stacey acted like nothing was wrong. I started to cry. It was unbelievable to me that he could see his own brother in need of help but do nothing. I was scared to stay at his house. Stacey had to work at the club that night and I begged him to let me go but he said he wanted me to stay at the house, so I did. I went in Stacey's room and locked the door and cried myself to sleep.

Steve quit his job at the University about a week later. I overheard a conversation between Stacey and his mom talking about Steve being in the hospital for a few weeks. Stacey told me his brother just had a mental breakdown, but I always felt like it was more to it. One day Steve came home from the doctor's office and had the biggest smile on his face.

"Why the big, cheesy smile, man? I asked.

He said, "I can hear now. The voices are gone."

I looked at him, confused but chose not to talk about it.

"That is great news! Congrats!" I said.

I immediately walked away to replay what I heard. Stacey did not seem to be moved by Steve's statement. I hated that Stacey didn't think what his brother said was strange.

"Your brother said he heard voices and now they are gone! You don't think something is wrong with that?" I asked.

"Calm down and stop trying to make a mountain out of a molehill," he replied.

So I kept my mouth shut even though it bothered me so much that he never seemed to care about anything.

PART 3

THE ROAD BACK

CHAPTER 10

THEN THE TRUTH COMES OUT

The truth will set you free. Well, not so much for me. The truth could have slapped me in the face with a brick and I still wouldn't have recognized it. I had enough signs piled up in front of my face but did nothing with them. I even had the good ole intuition that the Lord has blessed us women with, but it still didn't matter. I wasn't sure what it was going to take for me to walk away from this horrific relationship. Despite Stacey's inappropriate behavior, he still gave me something that I needed. He held me at night like he loved me. He gave me comfort at times. This only happened on his terms but when he decided to show love, I was in heaven. He would give me a kiss when I was asleep. Stacey did all of the things my mom didn't do for me. He made me feel like he truly cared with a simple touch. My mother and I didn't touch often. No kisses, no hugs. Even when she began to do these things as an adult, it felt completely awkward. Stacey did these things and it made me feel special. I felt wanted. The only thing was, two minutes later he would say things to me that would totally contradict his actions.

At this point, I was checking Stacey's phone all the time. Any chance I could get I would go through his text messages and emails to see what woman he was talking to and what lies he had told me. I came across a text to his ex-girlfriend Staci. He had always talked so bad about her. He told me how he wanted to spend his life with her and how she left him in the cold and moved to New Jersey without him even knowing. He made me feel like she was the worst person on the face of the planet. So it was shocking when I saw a text message asking her if she would ever consider marrying him. He confessed how in love he was with her and how he wanted to work things out. Once again, I was devastated. Everything was great with Stacey and I. It had been two weeks with no arguments and no evidence of him cheating. Well, no evidence that I could find. So I did something that I had not done in a long time. I wrote a poem about my current feelings, recorded it on video and posted it on YouTube and Facebook for the world to see.

LOVE'S BIOPSY

As I prepare for this microscopic examination,

I station myself close to the one who I love most, but yet far

From the clouds so everything is clear,

What I see and what I hear or heard.

See this love thing is more than just a word.

Under the light, I see your anatomy is grey.

And I'm so black and white that I immediately knew it

Wasn't right having to fight for that proper diagnosis that day.

You are so obtained.

So I scrape the surface of your heart, this was the critical part,

Slightly peeling back to reveal the real you.

But the you that I want is tied up in "confused."

Amused is what I ain't.

When the test results came back I almost fainted

when the Doctor said, "Miss, your relationship has a tumor.

Not one but two. And no humor can distract me from the feeling that's inside me seeing what's in front of you.

You still love her.

And if that is the case, then my love has been a waste unless

You are willing to start treatment today?

Your lack of feeling, no dealing, has me wondering what

Exactly what you are willing to endure to ensure that we last.

Willing to give up that blast from the past? No.

Well I was just giving you the opportunity to show your love for me

Cause I think everyone should know.

Even if it's just a drop, it can grow.

So stop telling me what I want to hear and tell me something I don't already know.

If it's not me you want then tell me you want more.

Fuck patience. How do you feel like you've cured me but I still have

Complications, love sick, worse than any radiation. Until their love

has ceased and your love for me has increased.

You are formally discharged...released.

I started looking at Stacey's ex-girlfriend's Twitter after that. Checking to see if she was tweeting him or saying anything that would lead me to believe that they were still dealing with each other. I saw two things that stood out that day. She talked about a book called *"Getting The Love You Want."* Stacey had just mentioned that same book to me the week prior and told me how it had changed his life. He said it taught him how to love better. One other thing she tweeted was, "I love your poetry." I knew then she had seen my YouTube video. This means she was checking out my page too. I just felt in my heart that we needed to connect somehow. I just wasn't sure how to reach out to her without Stacey finding out. A day later, I sent her a Facebook message and said, "I feel like we should talk." I later found out that she has also tried to reach out to me through my work email but her message went to spam. I gave her my number and she sent a text confirming that I would chat the next day at 4:00 pm.

I was sitting in the basement doing Stacey's nails before he went to work. His ex-girlfriend sent me a text to confirm our conversation and Stacey saw her name pop up on my iPhone.

"Who is that? Is that my ex, Staci?" he asked.

I said, "Yeah. She had a question about something."

I really had no clue what to say. I was obviously caught and I am a horrible liar. He didn't say any more about it. I finished his nails and he left for work.

The next day I took Stacey to the convention center where he had to DJ for three hours. There was a big expo going on that weekend which meant he would be totally preoccupied and I would have plenty of time to talk to her. I called her at exactly

4:00 pm.

"I just want to have a real woman to woman conversation," she started.

I told her I was down for that so she began. She told me how she had heard through her friends in the city that I was dating Stacey even though he denied it. He said we were just good friends. She told me they had gotten back together once she moved but her relationship with him had just ended in March when she found out about Tori. Apparently, he was cheating on her with Tori for about a year prior to us dating. He denied anything was going on. She also knew about Camille, Brianne, Carmen, Danielle, and even had a talk with Gina too who lied and told her that she did not sleep with Stacey but later found out that she did. Stacey somehow convinced Gina to lie to Staci about their relationship. My heart started to sink. I asked her how she knew about Camille and I mentioned that I heard that both Stacey and his best friend Mike had been involved with her. She went on to stay that one weekend Stacey came to visit her . She caught the train to work and he wanted her to be able to listen to music on his iPod while she rode on her long train ride. While she was on the train listening to music she also went through his pictures on the phone. There she saw pictures of Stacey having sex with Camille and Danielle. The description of the pictures was graphic. She said she wondered who was taking the pictures. She confronted Stacey about the pictures and he said that they were old. She pointed out the brand new diamond earrings in his ears that she had just bought him for Christmas. He was speechless. She went on to mention how she couldn't understand why he would even give her the iPod knowing those pictures were on there. It just didn't make sense. Nothing did.

She went on to tell me how Stacey asked her to go on a trip with him in two weeks to Dallas. During the summer he asked me to go on this same trip with him. Every year he would go out of town to DJ at this big convention. This particular year it was in Dallas. He said he would purchase my ticket if I wanted to go. We stayed on the internet for over an hour trying to find good ticket prices. He told me he would have it purchased in a few days. A week later he told me that his friends don't feel right having me there because it had always been a "guys" trip. I thought it was a little awkward and

I felt disappointed. Now I was finding out that he lied and actually planned to take his ex-girlfriend.

My conversation with Staci lasted for a few hours. We talked about him crying all the time.

"What did he tell you? Let me guess. He told you that he is bipolar?" she said.

"Yeah," I replied.

She went on to say that she believed it was something much worse than that. We talked about all of his women and all of his lies. I found out the times when I was waiting for him in the car for over 45 minutes after he got off work from the club that he was actually on the phone talking to her. He would tell me that he was waiting to get his check from the club owners. The night of the Kentucky Derby party when I was wondering why he was outside smoking for hours. He was talking to her. The smoke was starting to clear and the sight in front of me was not pretty at all. She told me about a time that they got into an argument about him not taking out the trash and he stormed out the door, got into her car and wrecked the car while backing out. She said he never said a word and when she asked him about it he blamed her for it.

It was her fault for nagging and making him mad. He never took accountability for anything.

After talking to his ex, I began to see the pattern. I didn't feel like she was saying anything out of spite. I felt like she genuinely cared about my well-being. She said she asked some of her friends about me and they all said I was sweet and that this was the only reason she reached out to me. She didn't want to see another victim. It was too late. Stacey had me tightly wrapped in his web and I could barely breathe. Before we got off the phone, Staci asked what I was going to do. I really wasn't sure. I didn't even think that he was owed a conversation. I wanted so desperately to leave him forever and hope that he would disappear from my life. I told her I wasn't sure how to handle the situation but that I wasn't going to let him know that we had spoken to one another. So, I told her I appreciated the talk and to pray for me.

I walked upstairs to see Steve standing in the kitchen making a sandwich and I told him this would be the last time he would see me. "Your brother is a habitual liar and disgusts me." I told him as I stormed out of the house.

Steve just shook his head and chuckled as I left. I was supposed to pick Stacey up from work but instead I sent Stacey a text message telling him to find his own way home. Then I turned off my phone so that he couldn't contact me. I kept this sick feeling in my stomach for a few days.

Days later I received a text message from him:

[I need help.]

He told me that he was willing to do anything and he didn't want to lose me. He asked if I would come over his house after work to talk. I did want to hear what he had to say and what he was going to recommend as a solution. I went to his house and we had a chat about our relationship and he told me that he wanted me to go with him to therapy.

I told Stacey it worried me that he would get into these dark moods where he wouldn't sleep, he wouldn't talk to anyone and all he did was just stare at the computer screen all day and night. I told him cheating with all of these women was out of control, too. One minute he was up and ready to take over the world and the next he was a completely different person. He eventually told me that he had a serious problem. He mentioned that he hadn't seen his therapist for over six years since his relationship ended with a woman named Dana who no longer lived in the city.

I encouraged him to start his sessions back up because he obviously needed some help. He complained about not having insurance and how the cost was over $100. I offered to pay and after a week he went. After his first session, he said he was so relieved and felt good that he had decided to go back. The next session he asked if I would attend. Before I agreed to go, I sent a text to his ex-girlfriend saying that Stacey waned me to go with him to therapy. "I think he really has a problem and needs help," I told her. She told me to run. She said that Stacey also asked her to fly in from New Jersey to attend a therapy session.

She kept saying that if I go I would be making a mistake and that I would stay trapped in his web. I wish I would have listened.

That day, we walked into this older building downtown and got on the elevator that seemed to be made for only three people at a time. As we walked down the hall, I started to get butterflies. I had never gone to a therapy session before. I didn't know what to expect. It was an older Caucasian woman who opened the door. She seemed very sweet, yet reserved. A little awkward to see her talking to a guy who lived such a hip hop lifestyle. Picture Mrs. Doubtfire talking to Kanye West. They just seemed so completely opposite. Before she started, she told me that it was a huge deal for Stacey to even want me to be there. It was a milestone, she said. She continued on to say that I should know that Stacey must really care about me if he asked me to be there. She then asked us about our relationship.

I told her I wanted to understand more about his illness. What is bipolar disorder?

"Did Stacey tell you that he was bipolar?"

Before I could answer myself, Stacey said, "She thinks that I am bipolar."

Clearly, I remember the conversation of him telling me that he was bipolar but I never opened my mouth to say anything about it. I didn't want to embarrass him. She told me Stacey is not bipolar. He has what is called Major Depressive Disorder. She went through a list of characteristics that did fit him to a T but still there was a part that was missing.

Stacey interrupted, "She thinks I am a sociopath too."

The woman laughed aloud, "No. Stacey isn't a sociopath."

She began to run down the list of what characteristics a sociopath possesses. The first characteristic is "charming."

Yep. That sounds about right.

"They are arrogant and believe they are superior to others."

I just shook my head in agreement.

"They have no discipline so they don't do well paying bills, finishing tasks, etc.," she said.

I couldn't help but immediately think about Stacey's rent not being paid on time and the day his electricity was cut off, his complaints about a credit card bill from college that he still hadn't paid despite just spending thousands of dollars he had spent on new furniture and equipment. "They lack remorse and lack empathy," she continued.

I almost started to tear up and then she said they almost always have a criminal history. Whew. I let out a sign of relief. Well he couldn't possibly be a sociopath because he had never gone to jail or had any criminal issues that I had known of. Despite her giving six other characteristics that fit him perfectly, I decided she was right and I tossed the thought out of my mind. She spoke about Stacey's ex-girlfriend Dana who had moved to Virginia after their breakup. She made Dana out to seem a little scary. She said she wasn't a good person. She even said the same about Stacey's ex Staci that I had spoken to recently.

I couldn't help but wonder how she could come to these conclusions when she had only heard Stacey's side of the story. She was the professional, so I listened. We talked about Stacey's affairs and she had quite an interesting theory. She said Stacey looks to sex as a comfort place just as when someone is upset they may go drink or do drugs.

It was almost like she somewhat agreed that I was the cause of his cheating. She said Stacey had a problem with abandonment that stemmed from his father leaving him. She told me when I say, "I am done" and leave his house, he feels abandoned and this is why he ran to those other women. Stacey shook his head in agreement the entire time.

The therapist asked us to do a homework assignment. She asked him to tell all the woman that he had a girlfriend. I believed most of the women already knew he had a girlfriend. She also asked me to not leave his house when he had an issue. Instead, try to resolve it in a calm manner. I offered to give it a try. There were so many other things I could have and should have mentioned. I never talked about the anger, the put-downs, and all the other weird things that didn't make sense. I'm not sure really why I never spoke about those things. I guess it was fear. After going to the therapy session with Stacey, I didn't talk to his ex-girlfriend Staci until later that year. He asked me to never call or text her. Since I was so determined to make the relationship work, I did what he asked.

CHAPTER 11

CALLING IT QUITS

My birthday was coming up and I had planned an entire birthday party at my favorite club, Oxygen and some of my close friends from out of town were coming in to celebrate. My best friend hated Stacey. She didn't even live in the same city but she could tell how I had changed for the worse and she didn't like it at all. My birthday fell on a Friday night, but my party was set for Saturday. On my birthday, I woke up to Stacey singing Happy Birthday and I was curious to see if he had any special plans for us. He handed me a half-open box of headphones and said "Happy Birthday." I was a little confused. The box was open and the headphones had to be the most generic headphones you could buy. I told myself to just be grateful but I couldn't help but think of the $300 I spent on a certain laptop stand that he begged me to buy for his birthday and to receive a $25 pair of headphones just didn't add up. Nevertheless, I was still hopeful that he had something planned. I saw him getting dressed and ready to leave and I said, "Wait. I will go with you." He convinced me that he didn't have time to wait on me to get dressed, so he left, saying he had errands to run. It was about 11 AM. when he left in my car. He didn't return back home until almost 2 AM. the next morning. I was asleep when he came home, completely drunk. I asked where he was and he had a long story about helping a friend who was in trouble. It was always something.

The next day was the big party. I told Stacey that all my girls were coming to the house to get dressed and he was furious. He said, "I don't need your nosey friends going through all of my things! They don't even like me so why are they coming over?" he yelled. He also mentioned that they would see him getting into a cab and make fun of him because he doesn't have a car. He was so irrational. My girls arrived just as his taxi pulled off. He was right about one thing. They didn't care about him at all. We got dressed and as we were walking up the stairs from Stacey's dungeon, one of my friends fell down the stairs. As she fell, another one of my friends from upstairs yelled, "OH NO! I locked my keys in the car!" My friend Rasheeda said, "This house is possessed. I can feel it!" While she seemed to be joking and everyone just chuckled as we called a locksmith and put ice on my friend's ankle, I couldn't help to believe that it probably was true. There was a disturbing energy in that house that never went away.

We arrived at the party and the minute I walked in, I saw Carmen. Then I looked to the left by the DJ booth and there was Camille. At my birthday party. I walked over to Stacey and asked "What are your girls doing at MY party?" He said, "It's open to the public right? I invited a lot of people." I was humiliated but I put on my smile and tried my best to have fun with my friends. All the while, on the inside, I was angry and hurt.

It was a Sunday. I had been at Stacey's house cleaning all day. He sat in the basement on his computer looking like a zombie as always. I had told him earlier that my close friend, Kim, had an engagement party that I planned to attend at 8:00 pm and I wanted to stop by my friend Sarah's house first for her sex toy party at 7:00 pm. Luckily, Sarah lived right around the corner from Stacey so I could pop in and out and then head over to Kimberly's party. So I got dressed around 6:00 pm and was getting ready to head out of the door around 6:45 when Stacey insisted on having his contact lenses for work. Since Stacey didn't have a car and his brother was gone, I would have to use my car. I asked him why he waited to say something until it was time for me to leave. Wal-Mart was on the other side of town and he would need them before 9:00 pm. I looked at my watch. He said he didn't think about it. He never thought about anything other than himself. He really didn't care that much for Kim because I had expressed to him that she wanted me to leave him alone. So I went to Sarah's toy party for only five minutes. I was disappointed that I couldn't stay because I would have to go to Wal-Mart before the optical store closed at 8:00 pm. I made it right on time; it was about 7:45 p.m. when I got there. First, the lady working in the optical center couldn't find his name in the system. When she did find it, the cash register wasn't working correctly. Needless to say, I left the store at 8:45 pm and I hurried to Kim's engagement party in which I arrived very late. I then had to leave early to get back to Stacey's house so he could have his contacts by 9:30 p.m. I walked into his house disappointed. Stacey simply thanked me and told me he was ready for me to take him to work. I took him to work and as soon as he got out the car and shut the door, I cried.

There were so many times that Stacey had kept me from my friends.

A week later, there was a big poetry night at one of the art museums in town. It was my first time doing poetry live in over 7 years. Life caught up with me and I forgot about the things that I really enjoyed. I even wrote a poem about Stacey. I wanted nothing more than for him to be there to hear it. The poem was about how people were always trying to break us apart and how our love was too strong for them to break us down. He told me he would be there. I looked at the door all night waiting for him to walk in. He never did. I sent him a text message asking him if he would make it and he replied back saying he would not be able to attend.

It was like he was responding to a co-worker who asked him to hang out for drinks or something. He saw me working on this poem for weeks. He knew how much it meant to me. I expressed it. He didn't care. He never cared.

I was too afraid of being insulted to call him, so I sent him a text. I told him how he hurt me, and that him not coming to support my poetry night when he knew how much it meant to me was wrong.

He responded, "Nobody controls what I do. You aren't my momma."

I couldn't even reply. What grown man even responds like that? At that moment, I knew it was time to call it quits. My friends were distant from me. I found myself crying all the time because he was so mean and belittling. Every other week, I found out that he was cheating with one of the same seven girls that he had been cheating with for the entire time we were together. I had to leave.

He tried to text me the next day. I didn't respond. He showed up for work the day after, walked into the studio and pushed everything off of the console and walked out the room. I was scared. He had these outbursts of rage and anger that came out of nowhere. He was good for throwing things. Once before, we had an argument in my office and he pushed everything off my desk. He was like a little kid that didn't get his way. I always thought he would hit me. A big part of me wishes that he would have so people would have something to see. Without the bruises, no one could understand the pain, the torment, and the mental and emotional abuse that I was going through.

Before walking away completely, I needed to get my stuff out of his house. He had already asked me for my key back after the Miami trip and I had returned it. So, I just had to hope that his brother was at home so I could get the things that belonged to me. Luckily, his brother was home and allowed me into the house. I got most of the small things that were important to me. Some things I couldn't even carry like my painting that hung on his wall downstairs. I had to suck it up. The only other thing that I wanted back so badly was my diamond ring.

I would often wear my old wedding ring when I was out with Stacey so that I could convince people that we were serious. I was so insecure. I felt it was the only way to keep women away from him. A few months prior, a friend and I decided that we would go to the club where Stacey was DJ'ing. I saw one of the girls that that he was known to be sleeping with and I made sure that she saw my ring when I ordered my drink. I could tell that she was very upset. A week later, I couldn't find my ring. I searched everywhere. I remember that last time I had it I put the ring in my glove compartment in the car. I asked Stacey if he had seen it and he told me no. He even went so far as to ask me if I had checked certain places like my car or my jacket pockets. I checked my only jacket at his house. I kept one small leather jacket at his place and I checked all the pockets twice to make sure that it wasn't there. I remembered very specifically putting it in the glove compartment in my car. Stacey had been the only other person in my car, however, he denied ever seeing the ring. While at his house picking up my things, I saw my leather jacket. When I lifted it up, my ring fell out of the pocket. It was if I had never checked the pockets at all. He had the ring the whole time.

I have no clue what he had intended to do with my ring. But I'm sure that he took it because he was upset when the girl told him that I was wearing a ring.

I called my dad and told him that I wanted to see him. I drove a few hours away, eager to receive advice from my father. As soon as my dad gave me a hug, I broke down into tears. I told him how I really loved Stacey but I didn't understand why he treated me that way. I was very close to my dad and always felt comfortable being transparent with him. I told him everything. I told him about the manipulation, not being able to spend time with my friends, the cheating, etc. My father pulled me close and asked me to have a seat next to him on a bar stool.

"Baby girl, I want you to listen to me. You have been dating a sociopath for the last year. He has abused you. I need you to get some help."

I didn't want to believe what my dad was saying. I couldn't have been in an abusive relationship for a year and not know it, could I? That night when I got home, I remembered the conversation I had with Stacey's therapist about sociopaths but I couldn't remember the characteristics so I looked it upon the Internet. Irrational thinking, insincerity, unreliability. Incapacity for love, superficial charm. My dad was right. From that point on, my father called me every day. He could see that I was becoming very depressed. He begged me to call a women's abuse group to get help but I kept telling him that I could not attend something like that because people would recognize my face. I was in denial that anything was wrong with me. In the meantime, Stacey continued to text me. This time, I really ignored him.

CHAPTER 12

INDEPENDENCE DAY

At the end of your AA meetings when you receive your coin that reminds you of how far you have come, I believe this should exist for people who have finally found the strength to leave an abusive relationship. After all, you too have dealt with a tremendously hard situation and you overcame it! I remind myself of how strong I am. I take the time to remind myself of my self-worth and how far I have come on my journey. Some people look at this as giving him power by focusing on the situation that happened but this is no longer about him, it's about me. This was a day that I claimed my victory. The day God gave me the strength to say, "NOT ANYMORE!"

I claimed December 19th as my Independence Day. I freed myself from Stacey. This was the day I decided that I deserved much better. But it wasn't easy after the breakup. More drama began to come my way. In one of my many attempts to finish college, I decided to take classes at a local university. My very first day of school I received a phone call from Stacey's sister, Wanda.

"You know I really liked you. I never had any problems with you but my brother is over here in my mother's arms crying about all the bad things you said about him and you calling him the devil."

She was referring to a conversation that I had with Stacey months ago before we even broke up.

She continued, "You don't know how much you hurt him!"

I couldn't believe it. My first day of class and I'm actually in the hallway having a yelling match with Stacey's sister. It was always amazing to me how dramatic Stacey could be at the drop of a hat. He could easily convince everyone around that he was the victim.

"I don't believe that my brother is perfect in any way. Nobody is perfect. Everybody makes mistakes. Why don't you just leave him alone?" she went on.

He told her that I was harassing him. I heard in the past she may be bipolar so I didn't feel the conversation was worth continuing. It seemed as if everyone in his family had some type of personality disorder. I told her that I appreciated her calling and her expressing her opinion. I also assured her that I had not and would never contact her brother again.

Things started to get ugly at work. We had never had a problem the entire year we were together. We kept it professional at work. I would like to think that I am an actress. When I turn on that microphone, I become happy and full of fun regardless of my situation. If we were having issues, we would just not speak. No one would have been able to tell. But after the breakup, things quickly changed. Two days later, I brought him a bag of his things that were left at my house and he wouldn't take it. He yelled, "FUCK YOU!" in the hallway and walked away. I don't think he could handle the lack of control. I think he finally understood that it was really over this time.

As time went on, strange things started to happen. I would see his car outside of my house, just sitting there. My doorbell would ring and by the time would get to door, no one was there. I would log onto Twitter and half of my messages from people with no profile picture would be speaking about DJ Spectrum for some reason. He was stalking me.

I eventually had to talk to my boss about it because it was getting bad. He brushed it off as if it wasn't a big deal, but I assured him that something needed to happen. He asked me if I was egging him on. I couldn't believe what I was hearing. It shouldn't have surprised me that he would take his side since they were fraternity brothers. At one point, every time I had an appearance, he was there. He showed up to a charity bowling event that he would have never attended in the past. He wasn't a social person at all. Despite being a DJ, Stacey was an introvert. And he certainly could not care less about the community. I walked out of the bowl-a-thon early and walked to my car. His car was parked right next to mine. All of the parking spots available and he parked right next to my car. I got in quickly and drove off without even looking. The next day, my boss pulled me to the side.

"I think I know what you are talking about now. I saw Stacey walk in to the bowling alley and walk right back out. He didn't even speak to anyone," he said.

He had no reason to. He was only there so that I would see him. That was it. I had no choice but to file a harassment claim. I called our corporate office and spoke to Human Resources about my situation. A full report was filed and I was informed that Stacey would be notified. A few days later, I was informed that Stacey had filed a counterclaim. He said that I showed up at one of his events that he promoted on a Friday night. It wasn't even his event. This man scared me. Why would I show up at his event? A promoter named Danny put the actual event together. I called Danny and asked to meet with him to tell him what was going on and to request that he send corporate a letter to confirm my story. We met at a local coffee shop and I told him the whole story. Little did I know, he was good friends with two of Stacey's ex-girlfriends, so he knew about his manipulation and abuse. He also told me that he went to middle school with Stacey. He said he remembered Stacey killing birds and putting them on people's cars. What Danny described happened to be another characteristic of a Sociopath.

Danny also talked about other incidences that happened more recently like records from other DJ's coming up missing as well as certain equipment. He said all of the DJ's believed Stacey stole their stuff but they couldn't prove it. I know the feeling. Stacey seemed to be a pro at deceiving people. He had been doing it for so long that he had gotten really good at it. Danny agreed to write the letter to HR to confirm that the event I attended was in fact NOT Stacey's event but his event and even agreed to speak a little to Stacey's character.

It was all in vain; after I followed up with HR, I was told my claim was dropped because there wasn't enough evidence that either one of us was harassing the other. I was blown away. This man was making my life a living hell and there was nothing I could do. Even though the claim was dropped, Stacey was removed from my show. He was no longer able to be in the building at any time when I was there. Once he showed up while I was working and our GM had to firmly ask him to leave.

For weeks I saw his car in the parking lot next door to the radio station when I got off work. He wasn't going to stop.

CHAPTER 13

THE HELP, THE HEALING AND THE HOPE

Everyone needs help. Each person's needs may be different but at some point we will all need to reach out our hands and ask for assistance on something. For some, that need is counseling or therapy. I can't for the life of me understand why the urban community frowns on therapy. Is it because we have been taught to not share our business with strangers? Or is it because we have been taught to "Pray about it honey!" I understand both points but it's so important to take a look at the situation as a whole. Sometimes we need to step outside of the picture to see it from a different perspective. We go to the doctor when we sprain our ankle. We can admit that fixing a sprained ankle is nothing we should try to do ourselves, right? We go to the doctor when we feel a lump on our breast. We want to make sure that it isn't cancerous and we understand that only a doctor can determine this. So why then, when we are depressed or when we realize something isn't right with how we are thinking or feeling, don't we want to go to a therapist? After all, our brain is the most important organ in our body. It controls everything. A therapist helps us to understand what is going on in the brain. They bring up the issues from the past that we didn't know existed that help us to deal with our current issues. I'm an advocate of therapy. I went to therapy for almost three years and it changed my life for the better. I learned how to love myself which is something I had never done before.

My first therapy session was quite interesting. We talked about why I was there, my current condition and how she could help. She was a very nice lady and I had really looked forward to chatting with her, however she didn't accept my insurance. I was so disappointed. I couldn't afford to pay $95 a session, so she recommended some other doctors and I eventually found the perfect fit. She also gave me the name of a psychiatrist. She told me that I might want to consider medicine because my condition was not so good. I had lost a great deal of weight in such a short period of time. I went from a size 8 to a size 2 in a matter of months. I couldn't eat anything. Everything I ate had no taste. I couldn't sleep at all. My mind was always on the move. I cried all day, every day. I would barely function at work.

My dad was adamant about attending my first session with the psychiatrist. I'm glad he was there. As soon as I walked into the lobby, the woman behind the desk called me "JJ" which means she knew exactly who I was. I was embarrassed. All I kept thinking was the wrong person was sitting on this couch.

I shouldn't be the one in so much pain when I had done nothing to deserve it. My father and I walked in to the office and I can remember being a little thrown off by the doctor's beat up leather couch and tons of elephants on his shelf. Although I was nervous and pretty pessimistic about seeing him, I still felt a warm feeling when I sat down. He asked me a ton of questions.

He asked me about the abuse and after every question he asked, "How do you feel about that?"

"Sad." I responded

I felt like the world was against me. No matter

how many wonderful people I had standing in my corner, I felt like the world was in darkness. My dad asked, "What can I do to help her?" He told him to continue to do exactly what he had been doing. "Just be there for her." The psychiatrist prescribed several different medications and asked that I continue to see him as well as my therapist.

I never pictured myself having to take medicine. It was really quite the struggle having to take five to six pills a day. I took medicine for anxiety, paranoia, depression and medication to help me sleep. Then the medicine of course had side effects. I suffered from bad stomachaches and headaches. But after some time, I can honestly say taking my medicine helped. It wasn't something that I was happy about. People at my church were saying, "You don't need to take medicine, you just need consistent prayer." I disagreed. I absolutely believe in the power of prayer; I also know that just like we take medicine for a headache, some people need to take medicine when other things are going on in his or her body. After the summer was over, I decided that it was time to wean myself off of the medicine. I heard some of the prescriptions I'd been taking were addictive. I didn't want to get to that point. So after a few months, I stopped taking all of my medicine once I talked to my psychiatrist.

I hate to sound so cliché but I felt like things would never be the same. I allowed someone to destroy who I was. My mind, my heart, my soul. I gave this man all of me. Every man I meet, I try not to be so suspicious of him but when he says certain things that Stacey used to say, or a feeling seems familiar, I just wanted to run. I haven't completely opened my heart to trust another man but at the same time in the past few years since my breakup, I haven't met a man worth my time and energy. The greatest lesson I learned from my relationship with Stacey was to listen to the voice in your head. God has blessed us women with intuition. It's that immediate thought: *This isn't right.* We try so hard to convince ourselves otherwise when we know we need to walk away. I saw the signs very early. The lies, the cheating, the odd behavior, the meanness. But I chose to focus on the good even though it clearly did not outweigh the bad. It's been years now, but it still feels like yesterday. Time has healed many of the wounds. I realized that emotional and mental abuse is real. I feel for the women who are now involved with him or the women that will soon come. No one deserves to be treated like that. No one.

When I first broke up with Stacey, I wanted to destroy his whole life. I thought of a million and one things that I could do to hurt him. Remember his house that was in foreclosure? I had thoughts of purchasing his home just to prove that I was in control now and I could make life hell for him. I even had people clear as day walk up to me and ask me what they needed to do to help "handle" him. I wanted him to hurt as bad as I did but then God spoke to me and let me know He would "handle" him. So I did the hardest thing I could do, I prayed for him. I prayed for him every night. I prayed for Stacey, his family, his other victims and his ex-girlfriends. Trust me, it was not easy. But it was a major step in my healing process. I had to move on with my life and as long as I held on to the anger and resentment I could never learn to love.

During this time, my boss was let go and an old co-worker of mine took over our radio station. She was an unfortunate witness to my everyday sadness. Some days when she was in town I would just cry in her office and tell her how much

I wanted to be better. I eventually had to break down the entire situation to her. She said she knew something was wrong with the guy when she met him. He avoided her like the plague but still discreetly harassed me in a way that no one could see. She told me that I needed to get myself prepared to leave the job. I did just that. I even proclaimed very single day, "I have to leave." I could only wonder if Stacey was the reason that two other past girlfriends moved away. One moved to New Jersey and the other to Virginia.

In September, I took a trip to Jamaica with two of Stacey's ex-girlfriends Staci and Lorraine. Yep. Really "Waiting to Exhale-ish." It was a well-deserved trip. I had spent the entire year crying every day, not wanting to get out of the bed. Not only did I gain the courage to get out of bed, I was able to finally throw away the grey hoodie that I wore almost everyday as a security blanket. Staci had finally cut off all communication with Stacey and Lorraine was now married to a wonderful man. Ironically, through us discovering each other we became accountability partners. We all entered the journey into hope, helping and healing after our relationships ended with Stacey. This trip was a breath of fresh air.

Staci suggested we go on this trip together. She was the one who told me a year ago to run. She also suggested that Lorraine come with us. Lorraine had been in a relationship with Stacey four years prior to Staci. Lorraine was very petite and gorgeous with long flowing curly hair. She was a vegan and the type to grow her own herbs, heavily into meditation and shopped at the thrift store for her clothes. Staci and Lorraine had known each other for a while. They met when they both found out that they were sharing a boyfriend.

While in Jamaica we really bonded. We sat on the beach joking about how weird Stacey was and talking about how hard it was to move past the things that he did. The ladies encouraged me to be strong. They had both been where I had been. They both understood the pain, anxiety, paranoia, and especially the depression. Although our situations were different, they were quite the same. Three women fell in love with a sociopath. We relaxed on the beach for a few days and shopped. Staci and I even bought a timeshare together! We all became great friends and it was just the beginning. While transferring flights to head back home, I received a phone call from my interim boss.

"How would you like to come to Houston?"

I responded, "I AM IN HOUSTON NOW! I CAN JUST STAY!"

Ironically, I was in Houston on a layover when she called.

She said, "I have a job for you if you would like it."

I immediately said, "YES!"

It was that moment I knew God was preparing me for greatness. I remembered the movie *EAT, PRAY, LOVE*. Julia Roberts' character, Liz Gilbert said, "You must be destroyed in order to be rebuilt." It was so true. I am an entirely new person and it was all because of this situation. I am stronger. I am more aware. I am a survivor.

It was a Thursday night in October. Lorraine and I just attended the Jill Scott concert. We had a wonderful time enjoying the great music. We were still kind of hype after the show and looking for something to get into. So she suggested we go visit her husband who was spinning at the club that night. We walked into the party; it was jammed packed full of people. As I walked to sit down on the couch, I could see Stacey from the corner of my eye. I also saw two of the women he had cheated on me with close by. Nevertheless, I shook my head with a slight smirk on my face and sat down with my drink. He made an effort to walk past a couple of times. It was his "thing." He had to be seen. One time he walked past and his hat got caught up in the Halloween decorations hanging from the ceiling. Some type of cobweb stuck to his hat as he squirmed to get out. The irony. I knew exactly what it was like to be caught in a web, but thank God I got out. We didn't stay at the party long. Just long enough to have a drink, allow my friend to share a dance with her hubby and catch the continuous stares from Stacey's women. I handled it well. I was very proud of myself. Had this been earlier in the year I may not have even been able to see his face without feeling sick to my stomach. As we walked out, my friend asked if I was okay.

"I am," I replied.

I was.

It was the last time I saw his face. I unfollowed

everyone on social media that was connected to him because I didn't want to accidently see him thanks to a repost or re-tweet. But I knew I had not reached my last step of healing. I still needed to forgive. It took me two years to really forgive him. I could not look past the pain he put me through. It hurt. But I had to recognize that forgiveness wasn't necessarily for him as it was for me. It wasn't until I read the book *The Shack* that I realized I had to forgive Stacey. I had to really consider that it was not him that hurt me, but yet the mental issues that Stacey possessed that created these situations. I also had to hold myself accountable for my part in it. I often ask myself what could I have done differently. One thing that I vowed to my friends was to listen to them when they share ill feelings toward a guy I am dating. I love my friends dearly and they all have my best interest at heart. I have to understand that sometimes other people see things that we don't. I also have a completely different outlook on mental illness. I dated someone with a mental illness. While my mother hasn't been professionally diagnosed, everyone in my family knows my mother has some type of disorder. My therapist believed that it could be Borderline Personality Disorder. This would explain her inappropriate and intense anger. However, we won't ever know because she has refused to get help. After cutting off every single person in the family, you would think she could see the common denominator. I saw the common denominator. The connection between Stacey and my mother.

"Jillian, have you ever thought about tattooing over your white patches on your hand? I'm sure you can find someone who can make it the exact same color as your skin."

I had heard those words before. This time it wasn't from Stacey, it was from my mother.

On Mother's Day, while driving to this fancy restaurant on the lake, my mother looked over at my hand on the steering wheel from the passenger seat. She looked concerned as she addressed my Vitiligo patches. I was shocked. She was unaware of my conversations with Stacey about my Vitiligo, which is what made her statement all the more piercing. My mother was saying the same thing to me that my abuser had said to me almost a year ago. I realized that my mother and Stacey were the same person and we would have to part ways. In order for me to fully heal I needed to let her go.

It was in this moment that I realized that my mother did not have the capacity to support me in the way I needed. While my friends were fasting and praying for me for weeks, she wasn't there. There was a point when my friend Kim showed up at my house at 4:00AM all because she felt in her spirit that I needed help. She was right. I ran to the door and on my way there I tripped over a plate with my daughter's ponytails sitting on it. As the doorbell rang over and over, I noticed the scissors that my daughter must have used to cut her hair while I was in my room crying for hours. Dad was very concerned about me so much so that he suggested I get help, attended my therapy appointments and called to check on me everyday. My life was in complete chaos; however, my mother could not see the magnitude of my complete depression. She simply felt that I was heartbroken and needed to get over Stacey.

Most people believe that mental disorders are pretty rare. But the fact is, an estimated 54 million Americans suffer from some form of mental disorder in a given year. Most people aren't prepared to cope once they find out that their loved one has a mental illness. It can be physically and emotionally exhausting.

According to Mental Health American, a mental illness is a disease that causes mild to severe disturbances in thought and/or behavior, resulting in an inability to cope with life's ordinary demands and routines. I now look at everyone as if they could have a mental illness. I mean what are the chances that we work with people who are bipolar but think, "Oh, she is just gets mad and overreacts sometimes." It could very well be more than just that.

Mental health problems may be related to excessive stress due to a particular situation or series of events. Depression is also considered a mental illness and on a scale from 1 to 10, I was at a 10.5 in my depression. The counseling was a major help and taking time for myself helped as well. Occasionally, I had to ask friends to watch my daughter when things seemed too overwhelming. It really helped to accept my feelings. I worried so much about what other people would think about me going to therapy. Once I started sharing with my friends what I had experienced and what I had learned about myself, I even inspired a few of them to start therapy. I was in therapy for about three years. We spent a great deal of time doing EMDR therapy which is proven effective for the treatment of trauma. It felt good to talk to someone who was unbiased. She was so comforting and caring. Never once did she not answer a call in the middle night when I thought I was going to take my life. Every now and then I feel the need to call my therapist and chat about my feelings on situations going on in my life. I gave myself permission to heal; healing takes time. I am so grateful for the experience; it has given me the strength I have today.

Your path to healing doesn't have to be long, winding and drawn out. Looking back on my experience, I want to be clear about the concrete decisions I made to move from a place of being broken toward becoming healed. I believe it is essential to:

1. End the relationship. There was no way for me to both heal and continue to be damaged at the same time. I had to cut off all contact from Stacey. No matter how much it hurts, you have to leave, believing that God wants better for you. God's best will come, but we cannot receive it until we let go of unhealthy attachments.

2. Tell yourself a different story about therapy and medicine. These are not evidence of weakness, they are tools to recover your strength!

3. Give yourself space (and grace) to heal. It took years for the damage to be done; it would take time for healing to take place.

4. Intentionally spend time with people who fully support your healing.

EPILOGUE

I'm sure you've noticed that some time is passed and may be wondering: What's she up to now? I ended my relationship with Stacey and set out on a journey to heal through a plan of self-care, treatment and counseling.

My wellness is a daily choice. I've learned so much from my experiences; and so much from my mistakes. I continue to activate a series of present choices to nurture wholeness and nourish me when I encounter present pain.

My well-being = my self-love. I have entered a space of creating self-love every day. This means I love myself enough to not allow any toxic people around me. I'm very conscious of what I feed my brain as well as my body. To love myself completely, I have a spiritual practice that includes prayer, serving and giving to my faith community, The Awakenings Movement.

Forgiveness has been essential. I have had to do the work of letting go of what was done to me so that I can be free to embrace what God has for me.

I am slowly and carefully dating again. Reflecting on who I was and what I allowed has made me more self-aware. When I choose to enter into one on one time with a man, I am very clear on my boundaries. The moment I detect any kind of abusive treatment, I quickly remove myself from the situation. I refuse to settle for anything less than what I truly desire in a mate, and the care I now know I both give and need.

God has given me such a desire to empower other women out of the overflow of what I have learned. I started the *I'm Me Foundation* as a way to redeem my experiences, and activate my lessons in the lives of young women. Many young girls are like I was, full of questions, talent and potential but without a caring mother to create an environment for their growth. We tour middle and high schools to teach workshops about beauty, fitness, maintaining personal health, and empowering them to be great! www.singlemomsrock.com is my offering to encourage women who are balancing motherhood, womanhood and working life.

I pray my journey through and out of that toxic relationship provides a light, some inspiration and some practical steps for you wherever you are on your path to joy, love and total health. It will be hard, scary and at times, lonely. Let me be a voice of encouragement from the other side of your pain: you can do it! I love you, and God does too.

"As soon as healing takes place, go out and heal somebody else."

– Maya Angelou.

RESOURCES

Many people think that if they're not being physically abused, they're not being abused. This couldn't be further from the truth. Here are some places to go for help.

BOOKS

The Emotionally Abused Woman: Overcoming Destructive Patterns and Reclaiming Yourself by Everly Engel, M.F..C.C.

Health scars of Emotional Abuse by Gregory L. Jantz, PhD.

The Verbally Abusive Relationship by Patricia Evans.

When Love Goes Wrong: What To Do When You Can't Do Anything Right by Ann Jones and Susan Schechter.

ORGANIZATIONS

Center for Relationship Abuse Awareness
555 Bryant Street # 272
Palo Alto, CA 94301
Women's Resource Center
1963 Apple Street
Oceanside, CA 92054
24-Hour Hotline (760) 757-3500

WEBSITES

www.betrayaltraumarecovery.org
www.hawc.org
www.healthyplace.com
www.stoprelationshipabuse.org
www.Womenshealth.gov
www.WomensLaw.org
www.verbalabuse.com
www.survivorswithvoices.org

ABOUT THE AUTHOR

Jillian "JJ" Simmons, a veteran radio host from Cincinnati, Ohio, is more than just another voice to fill the airwaves. As an on-air talent, she has captivated listeners from major cities from across the country. Over the years, she has interviewed many of the rich, famous and influential, including President Barack Obama. She has contributed her voice to the ongoing dialogue on the impact of Hip Hop on the American social and political landscape.

Having lost two uncles to AIDS, JJ is also a champion of AIDS education and awareness. She sits on the Board of Directions from AIDS Foundation Houston and even founded Red Tree Trees, an apparel company that uses Hip Hop infused tees as a tool of activism to emphasize the importance of getting tested.

In addition to being a positive influence on people she meets through her work, JJ is a proud mother of a beautiful daughter. She uses her passion for "the mommy experience" to motivate other single mothers through her network and website, Single Moms Rock. Although she has always had an innate desire to empower others, raising a daughter has deepened her desire to foster change in the lives of women, and inspired her to give birth to JJ's I'm Me Foundation. In keeping with her mission to create opportunities for positive social interactions and character-building experiences, JJ's I'm Me Foundation provides tools to improve the esteem and self-worth of girls and young women.

Made in the USA
Columbia, SC
04 September 2017